CLUB LEVEL DUPLICATE BRIDGE: WHICH STRATEGIES WIN?

by
Mark J. Routman, Ph.D.

Daring Books
Canton • Ohio

Published by Daring Books
P.O. Box 526, Canton, Ohio 44701

Library of Congress Cataloging-in-Publication Data

Routman, Mark J., 1944-
  Club level duplicate bridge.

  1. Duplicate contract bridge.   I. Title.
GV1282.3.R62   1986   795.41 '53   86-8825
ISBN 0-938936-44-1

Printed in the United States of America.

FOR:

BREE, DAVID AND TERRY

TABLE OF CONTENTS

ACKNOWLEDGEMENTS

If this were my seventh book, I suppose the list of people I'd like to thank would not be quite so long. However, it isn't my seventh, so the list is a bit long. First, I'd like to thank my partner (for most of this volume), Jo Ann Sanders, for allowing me to do this, for having a skin thick enough to withstand my abuse and the negative publicity about our game, for acting as my advisor and editor, and for encouraging me in this undertaking. Thanks, Jo. Also, Artie Kamien, Bucky Brooks and brother Lloyd helped by being my partner for two sessions each while Jo was away. Thanks, guys. And, of course, I'd like to express special appreciation to those in my local club who allowed me to note these hands during the evenings for the past year. Without their patience and permission, I could not have done this. Those who participated are listed below alphabetically:

Al Abide
Pauline Adelson
Bucky Brooks
Frances Cassanova
Travis Cassanova
Pansy Conner
Culver Craddock
Bobby Day
Nel Dedwylder
Evelyn Eason
Zeb Foster
Millie and Jim Gray
Dot Herrington
Artie Kamien
Ed Kossman
Frances Landau
Lacy Langford

Phil Lawes
Roche Lawes
Barbara and Doug Levingston
Helen Levingston
Vivian Levingston
John Meyer
James Potts
Bill Profilet
Virginia Rose
Billy Jo Ann and Joe Springer
Charlotte Turner
Bob Waller
Connie and Scott Warfield
Roberta Wiggins
Evelyn Wilkes
Gene Wynn

This is just a list of those against whom we played on these 52 hands. I would also like to thank the members of the club who are not listed but who allowed me to involve myself in this undertaking.

Terry (my wife), Leigh (Jo Ann's husband), Carol (my brother's wife) and Maureen (Bucky's wife) have all been very patient with their spouses and their spouses' passion — bridge. It must be hard for a non-player to understand how someone can become so engrossed in a deck of cards. They deserve special thanks. We sure appreciate it.

An additional note of thanks for their tolerance goes to Tom and Weezie, Tommy and Terry, Sarah and Bill, Sarah and Brent, Gayle and Jimmy, Jerry and Tina, and Sylvia and Marvin.

INTRODUCTION

In 1978, I joined the ACBL. At the time, all I knew was "vanilla American" and a bit of party bridge. I didn't even know that there was much complexity to the game. Then my brother Lloyd sent me a bridge book to read . . . which opened new doors for me. I began to read bridge books as fast as I could devour them and with as much time as my other activities permitted. Needless to say, my perspective about the game changed. The challenge of duplicate bridge fascinated me. The more I read and the more I played locally, the more I wanted to play tournament bridge. However, being geographically isolated and raising a family prevented as much of that as I would have liked. I found myself, therefore, playing most of the time at our local, once a week, non-expert game, and trying to improve my bridge. Fortunately, my partner, Jo Ann Sanders, was also interested in developing our game, so we began to add sophistication to our system, despite the local level of play. And yet, despite it all, we did not win all of the time. Most of the books I had been reading dealt with a level of sophistication nonexistent at the club level. Playing once a week at our local game was not like the Summer Nationals . . . no one even played weak two's.

There seemed to be a void of material which dealt with techniques to be used to win in local, non-expert games. It is that void which the present volume hopes to partially fill. For most duplicate bridge players who have little opportunity to attend tournaments, it is hoped that the present work will provide some "meaningful" reading material . . . which talks about the kinds of games they are likely to run into. Even for the tournament attender, local games are periodically visited, and this work may be of help.

A note about how the task of writing this text was undertaken. It seemed, in the reading which I had done, as though most of the hands discussed dealt with situations which rarely occurred. The hands which often occurred (by random deal) were seldom described. I, therefore, decided to write a book containing hands which actually happened. No hands, bids or anything else in this book are contrived. All of the hands appear as they actually happened, including mistakes made by me and my partner(s). Some of the hands are boring, some exciting . . . but all are real. What you are reading is a cross section of our local game. I have not even switched the hands to make myself declarer.

It is certain that many of the hands will be uninteresting (such as two level bids) and many poorly played, but that is not the point. This is a random selection of hands which we played over a one-year period. The point is this: What actually happens on the local level in terms of the types of hands played and the strategies necessary to win given those hands? This book may be more utilitarian than entertaining.

I expect that we will find that "slam" hands are rare, "game" hands less frequent than "partials," and that low level competitive bidding strategies largely determine who wins and who loses.

What I have done is to seat myself North-South each week for the first 26 weeks and then East-West for the final 26 weeks. This is an attempt to ensure that most of the people at our club will be confronted in this volume.

In order to ensure that all members of the club will be faced as opponents (because some pairs sit in the same seating position each week), I have described Board #1 on Week #1, Board #2 on Week #2 and so forth. Fifty-two boards will be described, which neatly comes out to be about one year's effort, and, at the same time, the number of hands typically encountered in two sessions at a regional.

The bidding and play of a particular hand follows in sequence as they occur. This is followed by a discussion of the results. I then describe the bidding and the play as they "should have" developed. Each hand concludes with lessons to be learned from that hand.

Then, after we have concluded the 52 hands (in terms of independent analysis) a summary of the lessons learned may provide us with some strategies which have the greatest probability of being successful. Following that discussion, the data will be approached in a different, more statistical fashion to see if there are some lessons to be learned that were not dealt with previously.

It is possible (given the type of training which I have had) to deal in somewhat complex fashion with these statistics. However, keeping in mind that many of those who enjoy bridge have not had this type of training, I will deal in terms of simple percentages. The average bridge player ought to be able to make some sense out of that, I feel. (We will be speaking in terms of trends and percentages rather than in terms of standard deviations, etc.)

I think a few words ought to be said about the terminology and abbreviations used. Most readers know this, I am sure, but for those who don't, LHO means left hand opponent; RHO = right hand opponent; K = king; Q = queen; J = jack; KC = king of clubs and so on.

I might also point out that for the first 26 weeks, Jo Ann was my partner, and for the next 26 weeks, also, except for 6 weeks. I had three different partners during that six-week period (Artie Kamien, Bucky Brooks and my brother Lloyd). I sat North for the first 26 weeks and East for the subsequent 26.

It is, incidentally, no crime nor shame to be labelled a non-expert. That doesn't mean you lack ability or that you have no talent. It means that you have spent your energies more than have the experts. You have not had the time nor been willing to devote the time necessary to develop the skills which would make you an expert.

Therefore, it is not with a disparaging eye that I look at our local game. As a matter of fact, I very much enjoy every one of the people with whom I play locally. And, it is a challenge . . . just of another sort (in terms of the types of strategies). The local game in which I find myself is the friendliest I have encountered, incidentally.

I think that the average reader of this volume will see that my local game is very elementary. Does that mean that the generalizations I make do not apply to your more sophisitcated game? Perhaps to varying degrees they do. If nothing else (and here the academic in me rears its head), the methodology developed here can be used to make generalizations about any local game or tournament. Perhaps that will be a future project of this author.

I. THE HANDS SITTING NORTH-SOUTH

1. A Weak Opener

Week 1
Board 1
No one vulnerable
North Dealer

Tonight we face a male sitting east and a female sitting west. They are not partners ordinarily, and neither plays a very sophisticated game. She does seem, though, to be a bit steadier than he is.

1. What Happened:

A. The bidding:

As dealer I pick up the following:

> North
> ♠ A J 7 6
> ♥ K J 10 2
> ♦ Q J
> ♣ 10 6 2

Twelve highs with 4-4 in the majors. Jo Ann and I play what is called "Variable Notrump." That means that with 12-14 highs and balance, non-vulnerable, we may open 1NT. Vulnerable, our range is 15-17. As I go into the tank, I think I'm a bit weak in the minors for that, so I open 1C. LHO (left hand opponent) doubles, Jo bids 1NT. It goes pass, pass, and LHO continues with two diamonds, where it dies.

The Bidding

N	E	S	West
1C	double	1NT	pass
pass	2D	all pass	

B. The play:

Jo Ann leads the four of clubs (How dare she lead my suit?). Dummy comes down with four highs.

North (me)

♠ A J 7 6
♥ K J 10 2
♦ Q J
♣ 10 6 3

West (dummy)

♠ 10 8 3 2
♥ 8 4
♦ 6 4 3
♣ A 8 5 2

Declarer plays the two from dummy and takes my ten

with his jack. (I think I've learned something from this hand already). Declarer continues with the king of clubs from his hand, all following. Then he plays the ace of diamonds and I drop the queen (which has no effect). He continues with the king of diamonds, all following. Finally, the ten of diamonds is played on which I pitch a low heart, after a pause. (I want a spade return from Jo and for declarer to play the hearts from his hand.) Declarer obliges with the heart ace. He follows with the nine of spades, which partner takes with the queen. She continues with the king, all following. She then plays the four of spades which declarer ruffs. Declarer exits with the three of hearts to my jack. I play the king of hearts, which holds, followed by the ace of spades, which is ruffed. Declarer's nine of hearts is then good.

The hands are then exposed:

North (me)
♠ A J 7 6
♥ K J 10 2
♦ Q J
♣ 10 6 3

West (dummy)
♠ 10 8 3 2
♥ 8 4
♦ 6 4 3
♣ A 8 5 2

East (declarer)
♠ 9 5
♥ A 9 6 3
♦ A K 10 7 2
♣ K J

South (partner)
♠ K Q 4
♥ Q 7 5
♦ 9 8 5
♣ Q 9 7 4

C. Results:

We had 7½ tables in play this night. The results on this board were as follows:

North-South Pair Number	Contract	Made	Down	North-South Points	North-South Matchpoints
1.	2DE	4		-130	2
2.	3DE	3		-110	4½
3.	1DE	3		-110	4½
4.	3CS		3	-150	½
5. (us)	2DE	3		-110	4½
6.	1DE	3		-110	4½
7.	1NTE	3		-150	½

We got a 4½ on a top of 6. Not bad . . . but did we deserve it?

II. What Should Have Been:

A. The bidding:

On the one hand, it is ordinary and positive for an author to start out demonstrating his competence in the area in which he is writing. (Would you want to read a book by someone who didn't know what he was talking about?) On the other hand, this is an honest book. The events really happened . . . even boring hands are included. It turns out that I was slightly less than perfect on this hand (try to be charitable and forgiving toward the author . . . after all, it is his book). Actually, North messed up on this one.

With twelve highs and no strong suit, North should not bid. Furthermore, the Q-J of diamonds may be of little value and should be discounted. Partner may be misled

16

about North's hand and may also get off to the wrong lead (as occurred). North may have an opportunity to enter the bidding later (by supporting partner or by balancing), but should not, in my opinion, open in first seat.

South's response of 1NT is a nice bid. It describes her hand point-wise and indicates the lack of a four card major, but with stops in the majors. In that sequence, I would prefer it.

B. The play:

I hope my skin is thick enough to handle the embarrassment of this one and the adverse publicity about my game that this hand might generate. Anyhow, I did it again.

East did not play the hand well at all. After a club lead, he could lay down the king of clubs, then the ace of hearts and out a heart. He could win the return (or ruff the third spade), ruff a heart, pitch a heart on the ace of clubs and draw trump for making four. As he played it, however, he gave North the chance to hold him to making two for a top.

East ruffed North's jack of spades at trick nine, producing the following four-card ending:

North (me)
♠ A 7
♥ K J
♦
♣

West (dummy)
♠ 10 8
♥
♦
♣ A 8

17

Declarer then leads the three of hearts from his hand which is taken by North's jack (west pitching a spade). North continued with the king of hearts which wins. The ace of spaces is ruffed and declarer's nine of hearts is good. All north had to do, after winning the jack of hearts, is lead the ace of spades for declarer to ruff, win the heart return, and North's seven of spades would be good. That would be a top on the board (making 2 for -90).

Lessons:

1. You need not be an expert to write a book (or perhaps even experts make mistakes).

2. East-West failed to capitalize on North's mistakes, and North failed to capitalize on East-West's mistakes ... a comedy of errors. Playing a steady game (and not even a brilliant game) would have gotten us a top here.

3. Bidding seems to have been important. When North-South competed to 3C, and did not get competition, they got a bottom. When East-West found notrump, they got a top. Both bidding and play were important on this hand.

2. A Major Error

Week 2
Board 2
North-South vulnerable
East Dealer

A couple of gentlemen greet us with smiles on this round. The East player is the same person who sat East last week but with a different partner. I take a peek at the following miserable collection, which makes me want to write down the next hand and to skip this one. But, if I did that, the hands wouldn't be random, so I'll suffer through. At least I won't have to concentrate on my hand as much and will have time to write down what happens.

North (me)
♠ J 10 2
♥ 10 9 7 6 2
♦ 4 3 2
♣ 7 2

Four deuces (I'm in the wrong game).

I. What Happened:

A. The bidding:

East opens the bidding with one club. Partner finds a double and West bids one spade. I'm off the hook, so I pass. LHO bids 2NT. Partner, vulnerable, bids three diamonds. Now, Jo Ann is basically conservative. She must have a rock. Especially since her RHO has shown power and some diamonds. She is saved by a three spade bid to her left which is raised to four spades by LHO. Jo doubles and all pass. (Someone obviously switched the bridge cards for pinochle cards).

The Bidding

N	E	S	W
	1C	Double	1S
pass	2NT	3D	3S
pass	4S	Double	all pass

B. The play:

I'm on lead. I pick a diamond. Rather than pick the four, and have to follow to the next trick with a lower one, indicating an even number, and rather than lead the "two", indicating an honor (by our system), I pick the three, intending to follow with the four and the "two." Dummy comes down with the following:

East (dummy)
♠ A 9 6
♥ K 5 3
♦ J 9
♣ A Q J 8 5

20

North (me)

♠ J 10 2
♥ 10 9 7 6 2
♦ 4 3 2
♣ 7 2

That accounts for some of the missing points. A distinct overbid was made, particularly with the double behind him. We have a fairly (being charitable) inexperienced club. The 9D is played from dummy and partner plays the AD. Declarer plays the five. The KD is continued, all following. Partner continues the diamonds with the Queen. She knows declarer has three from my count (up the line for odd number). The 6S in dummy takes the trick. Declarer leads the 9S off of dummy to his king, then the 4S to dummy's ace, partner playing the queen. That wouldn't be a falsecard (deliberately giving up a trick), so partner must have doubled 1C with only two spades. The JC is played from dummy and partner wins the king. I now know we, at least, have a one trick set. Partner plays AH and we have beaten it two tricks. The rest is irrelevant. The hands are exposed and, again, surprises.

North (me)

- ♠ J 10 2
- ♥ 10 9 7 6 2
- ♦ 4 3 2
- ♣ 7 2

West (declarer)

- ♠ K 8 7 5 4
- ♥ Q J 4
- ♦ 10 8 5
- ♣ 9 3

East (dummy)

- ♠ A 9 6
- ♥ K 5 3
- ♦ J 9
- ♣ A Q J 8 5

South

- ♠ Q 3
- ♥ A 8
- ♦ A K Q 7 6
- ♣ K 10 6 4

C. Results:

We had 6½ tables:

North-South Pair Number	Contract	Made	Down	North-South Points	North-South Matchpoints
1.	3SW		1	+ 50	2
2.	3SW		1	+ 50	2
3.	3SW		1	+ 50	2
4.	3CE*		1	+ 100	4
5. (us)	4SW*		2	+ 300	5
6.	3DS		1	-100	0

* = doubled contract

A top. Bidding four spades is a bit outrageous. Just the fact that they found their way to four is enough to get us a good board. Notice the double is worth only ½ matchpoint.

II. What Should Have Been:

A. The bidding:

Forgetting what East and West did or should have done, let's deal with how South should have contended with their auction so as to get the best board possible. If her RHO opens one club, as he did, a double indicates, to me, support for the unbid suits, particularly the majors (no less than 3-3 in the majors). Her partner would be misled about her distribution and may get off to the wrong lead. I would overcall one diamond. If her LHO then bids one spade and her RHO bids 2NT, she should pass. We're not going anywhere, and she has good defense against 2NT (we take five diamonds, a club, a heart and a spade (down three). To come in with three diamonds, vulnerable opposite a broke partner, may be suicidal.

Let's examine her double. First, she knows that (at most) East-West have 22 highs between them (actually 21). Most pairs won't get to 4 spades at our club on 22 highs, unless the hand is wildly distributional. If it is, she may expect a diamond void to her left, as her RHO bid notrump and she has five diamonds. Further, she has to discount the spade queen as it may be of little value. Therefore, if they make it they get a good board, period. If they don't, they get a bad board, period. And, the double may tip off the opposition. He may then figure South to have all the missing points and play the hand accordingly. Why double?

B. The play:

Nothing extraordinary happened. No comment.

Lessons:

1. The bidding was again important . . . much more important than the play.

2. Bidding to the three level, vulnerable against not, when your partner has not bid at all, would seem to be losing strategy.

3. Letting the opponents hang themselves sometimes pays off.

4. Doubling voluntarily bid games when your opponents lack the points for game is not necessary and may be counterproductive.

3. Only Two Points Short

Week 3
Board 3
East-West vulnerable
South Dealer

Another two gentlemen come our way this week. They are trying out new systems each week, but have not mastered the sytems they included the week before. But, at least they are trying to improve.

As the partner of the dealer I pick up these cards:

North
♠ K J 7 2
♥ Q 5 4
♦ J 5 3
♣ J 5 2

Eight highs and balance.

I. What Happened:

A. The bidding:

My partner opens with 1H. RHO passes. Jo Ann and I play a forcing notrump. That means that if I respond

1NT and then, following a two level minor bid by her, bid 2H, I show her 5-7 support points. If I instead bid 2H directly, I show her 8-9 support points, which I have. I therefore bid 2H. LHO passes and, after a hesitation, Jo bids 4H, which is passed out.

The Bidding

N	E	S	W
-	-	1H	pass
2H	pass	4H	all pass

B. The play:

Partner has to play this one, and I am dummy again. The 10D is led by partner's LHO. I spread dummy without comment.

Of course, I can't see partner's hand. However, for the sake of readability, I'll spread it now, and describe the play as partner apparently saw it. Dummy is North and declarer is South.

North (dummy)
♠ K J 7 2
♥ Q 5 4
♦ J 5 3
♣ J 5 2

10D

South (declarer)
♠ 10 9 5
♥ A K 10 7 2
♦ A K 6
♣ Q 10

Partner has 16 highs and balance. Again, the 10D is led. Without comment the play will be described. Partner covers the ten with the jack which is covered with the queen and she plays the ace. She leads the 2H from hand and wins the queen with both following low. The 4H is led from dummy and she wins the ace with both following. She continues with the king to draw the last trump and her RHO pitches the 2D. Then, she leads the 10S from hand which loses to the queen to her right. RHO returns the eight of diamonds. She grabs her king, all following. She then leads a spade from hand (the five) to dummy's king, which loses to her RHO's ace. Back comes the 9D which holds and wins, her LHO pitching the 7C. RHO switches to the king of clubs, which holds. The eight of clubs goes to the ace of LHO and partner is down two. Minus 100.

C. Results:

Strangely, there were seven tables in play, but only the results for six. We never did figure out what happened, but in terms of the overall score for the night, it made little difference. One North-South forgot to play the board, perhaps. In any event, it wasn't scored, and both the North-South and East-West pairs had left before we knew what had happened. This has never before occurred at our club that I am aware.

North-South Pair Number	Contract	Made	Down	North-South Points	North-South Matchpoints
1.	3HS		1	-50	2½
2.	2HS	2		+110	4
3.	2HS		2	-100	½
4.	4HS		1	-50	2½
5. Us	4HS		2	-100	½
6.	3HS	3		+140	5
7. No Score entered					

Note: Here the matchpoints were adjusted to base the points upon the six entered scores. Actually, the seventh pair received an average minus for the board.

We tied for bottom. The hands are finally exposed.

North
- ♠ K J 7 2
- ♥ Q 5 4
- ♦ J 5 3
- ♣ J 5 2

West
- ♠ 8 4 3
- ♥ J 8 6
- ♦ 10 7
- ♣ A 7 6 4 3

East
- ♠ A Q 6
- ♥ 9 3
- ♦ Q 9 8 4 2
- ♣ K 9 8

South (declarer)
- ♠ 10 9 5
- ♥ A K 10 7 2
- ♦ A K 6
- ♣ Q 10

II. What Should Have Been:

A. The bidding:

The question revolves around the logic of the 4H bid. I was known to have 8-9 support points. Partner had 16 highs and balance. She knows we have 24-25 points. If I had four pieces of hearts, I would have less outside strength because a point would be added for the fourth heart. Most say, I imagine, that 26 points are needed for a major suit game. But, a point or two away is not in and of itself a reason to stop short, if there is a fit in the off-suits and/or good distribution. However, partner has balance and a "soft" queen of clubs. We do, though, have a tool: a "help suit game try," which can be used. If she had bid 3C, after my 2H response (to see if I had a top honor in clubs so her queen might not be wasted), and if I did not have one, I could retreat to 3H, which she would pass. Possessing one of the top 3 honors, I would bid 4H. But, with no spade control, with balance, and 1-2 points short of 26, I feel she should pass 2H. Furthermore, as we now see, in questionable games, if this hand is representative, making a partial is good for a better than average board.

B. The play:

Partner had little or no control over the hand. The only thing which I would have done differently would have been to lead the 9S from her hand on the second play of spades instead of the five. That way, when the nine loses to the ace, if she ever regains control, she can go to the king and get a pitch on the long spade. Of course, this would never have materialized, as it was defended. But, at that point, she did not know she would get a club switch.

Lessons:

1. In questionable (close) games with non-experts, settle for a partial and a plus score.

2. The bidding of this hand was also more important than the play (in terms of determining the matchpoint result).

4. No Major Involvement

Week 4
Board 4
Both vulnerable
West Dealer

We've done pretty well the last two weeks, but tonight we had our troubles. We missed one slam due to a bidding misunderstanding, got fixed a couple of times, and fixed ourselves. We have an 8½ table game tonight and I peek at the following, sitting to the left of dealer (the male half of a married couple):

```
              North
           ♠ Q 4 3
           ♥ 10 4 2
           ♦ Q J 10 2
           ♣ K 4 2
```

Once again I have garnered my share of two's. Eight highs and a flat hand. Not very exciting. Looks like a nice dummy.

I. What Happened:

A. The bidding:

West opened the bidding with one club. I passed. LHO passed. Partner passes. I almost lost my teeth on that one. She must have a rock with clubs. She's got them. Good for her!

The Bidding

N	E	S	W
			1C
pass	pass	pass	

B. The play:

I make what I think is the usual lead of the queen of diamonds. Dummy appears with a perfect "pass."

North
♠ Q 4 3
♥ 10 4 2
♦ Q J 10 2
♣ K 4 2

East
♠ K 7 6
♥ 8 5
♦ 9 8 6 5
♣ 9 8 5 3

Dummy plays low to the first trick, partner the seven and declarer wins with the ace. The jack of spades is led by declarer, which is covered with my queen and won with dummy's king, partner playing the two. (That clears up the location of the fourth two.) A low heart from dummy is taken by partner with the ace. She fires back the four of diamonds, won by declarer with the king. Declarer then plays the king of hearts, all following. Then the nine of hearts, ruffed in dummy with the nine. Back comes the six of spades from dummy to declarer's ace. Then declarer leads the jack of hearts. I could ruff with the king, but instead I decide to save my good king and pitch my last spade (to perhaps overruff declarer). The three of clubs in dummy wins by ruffing the jack of hearts. The eight of clubs off dummy rides to my king. I play the jack of diamonds. Partner pitches the eight of spades. I continue with the ten of diamonds which partner ruffs with the queen of clubs and declarer overruffs and claims, making four. He lost a club, a heart and a diamond. Minus 130.

The hands are then exposed:

North
♠ Q 4 3
♥ 10 4 2
♦ Q J 10 2
♣ K 4 2

West
♠ A J
♥ K J 9 3
♦ A K 3
♣ A J 10 6

East (dummy)
♠ K 7 6
♥ 8 5
♦ 9 8 6 5
♣ 9 8 5 3

South (partner)
♠ 10 9 8 5 2
♥ A Q 7 6
♦ 7 4
♣ Q 7

C. Results:

It did not go too well for us on this one.

North-South Pair Number	Contract	Made	Down	North-South Points	North-South Matchpoints
1.	2NTW	2		-120	3½
2.	3NTW	3		-600	1
3.	2NTW	2		-120	3½
4.	1CW	3		-110	5
5. (us)	1CW	4		-130	2
6.	3NTW		3	+300	7
7.	3NTW		1	+100	6
8.	3NTW	4		-630	0

We get a "2" for our efforts on a 3½ average. The question is why?

II. What Should Have Been:

A. The bidding:

First of all, bridge is a game of percentages and probabilities. If you bid slams when you have a 75% chance, you will make your slam more often than not, though occasionally you will go down. One should not be influenced by the periodic "one chance in four" of going down (when it occurs) by assuming that in similar circumstances, therefore, one should not bid a slam. Playing the percentages will win in the long run, though not on any one particular hand. With that in mind, let's look at the bidding.

West, by opening 1C, gave North-South the chance to compete. He was allowed to buy the contract at 1C. North has no bid, nor does dummy (East). Should South bid? A case could be made for "pass", 1H, 1S, or "double." She chose "pass." South must assume, I believe, that West has no more than 21 points, and that East has no more than five, maximum. She has eight highs, which therefore marks North with no fewer than six. Probably, she might assume that East-West have between 22 and 26 points, with most concentrated, for sure, in the West hand. Therefore, North-South have between 14 and 18 points. That means that North has 6-10 points. It is possible, however, that North is trap-passing, just waiting for the double. If so, he may have as many as 19 points with a club stack. In South's position, though, I would assume that West is strong, but too weak for a two opener.

Let's examine South's options:

1. Pass. Let them buy it. This gives them the opportuni-

35

ty to play at the one level in their suit when you hold both majors. A penalty double of 1C becomes impossible. East-West have announced that they lack the points for game (especially when the points are so concentrated in one hand). Therefore, West is not given any chance to overbid.

2. One heart has the advantage (?) of lead direction. But, it is only four cards long. It may mean you miss a spade fit if it is passed out. Further, do you really want a heart lead when West may have to play it out of his hand because he can't reach dummy to take a finesse? However, it is still possible to retreat to one spade on the one level if doubled.

3. One spade. A five card suit, but lacking honors. He would have to retreat to the two level if doubled. Do you want a spade lead?

4. Double. This is my choice. A greater chance of finding a fit by doubling. We play a double of a minor shows preference for the majors, though some tolerance for the other minor. The advantage is that a fit is more easily located, with less chance, therefore, of a penalty double. If partner were then to bid diamonds, South could bid hearts (saying to North: take a choice between spades or hearts) or pass diamonds, as North's diamonds are probably strong. South could simply pass any bid made by North to indicate the nature of her balancing double.

Should West decide to intervene, nothing would be lost by North-South, as West would then be required to make more tricks in clubs or to play in notrump, with a probable major suit lead (and no ruffing power in dummy).

If South had lacked support for both majors, an overcall would certainly be preferable to a double, in my opinion.

I'm sure there is no unanimity on this one. In any event, passing 1C was not winning strategy on this hand, though that does not make it wrong in terms of percentages.

B. The play:

Nothing unusual occurred in the play of the hand. West played the hand well, and North-South made no blatant defensive errors.

Lessons:

1. Do not let them play one of a minor when you hold both majors.

2. On the local level, bidding seems to weigh heavily in terms of getting matchpoints.

5. Notrump with Balance

We face a couple of women on this round who are known for their unpredictability. I have been fixed by them many times before.

I. What Happened:

A. The bidding:

At last. A real hand.

```
                    North (me)
                 ♠  Q J 4
                 ♥  A 9 4 3
                 ♦  A K Q
                 ♣  K J 5
```

Balance and 20 highs. We play that a 2NT opener is 20-21 points. I qualify perfectly for that. With our opponents passing, partner responds 3H (which I alert).

That is a transfer to 3 spades. I obediently bid 3S. Partner bids 3NT in response, giving me the choice between 4S and 3NT and describing a hand with five spades rather than six. I pass 3NT after some thought.

The Bidding

N	E	S	W
2NT	P	3H(alert)	P
3S	P	3NT	all pass

B. The play:

LHO leads the six of clubs. Jo lays down a nice hand which she described well with her transfer and 3NT rebid.

North (declarer) . . . me

♠ Q J 4
♥ A 9 4 3
♦ A K Q
♣ K J 5

South (dummy)

♠ A K 9 8 7
♥ 6 5
♦ J 9 8 3
♣ Q 9

It looks as though those playing in 4S have a maximum of 6S (they must lose a heart and a club with a heart lead or just a club with any lead except a heart, as they will get a heart pitch on a club.). What about notrump? I count five spades, four diamonds, one heart and two clubs, with a club lead. With a heart lead it would be different, therefore making twelve tricks. That should be a good board and will even beat some of the pairs that may play 6S or 6NT and get a heart lead. The play was elementary. I cashed the A, K and Q of diamonds, then two spades from my hand (queen and jack, all following), then led the king of clubs. I can get back to my hand with the ace of hearts to make the last club, making 6.

C. Results:

We did get a 5½ on a 6 top.

North-South Pair Number	Contract	Made	Down	North-South Points	North-South Matchpoints
1.	3NTN	5		+660	3½
2.	3NTN	5		+660	3½
3.	5SS	5		+650	1½
4.	3NTS	4		+630	0
5. (us)	3NTN	6		+690	5½
6.	3NTN	6		+690	5½
7.	4SS	5		+650	1½

The hands are exposed:

North (me)
♠ Q J 4
♥ A 9 4 3
♦ A K Q
♣ K J 5

West
♠ 5 3 2
♥ K Q 8 2
♦ 4 2
♣ 8 4 3 2

East
♠ 10 6
♥ J 10 7
♦ 10 7 6 5
♣ A 10 7 6

South (dummy)
♠ A K 9 8 7
♥ 6 5
♦ J 9 8 3
♣ Q 9

II. What Should Have Been:

A. The bidding:

I finally get the opportunity to congratulate myself. Jo Ann did a nice job with the description of her hand and not pressing for slam, which was obviously not needed to get a good board. When the decision came as to whether to play in notrump or spades, several considerations made me decide to play in notrump. First, the "short hand" (the one with the least number of spades) had balance (no suit would be ruffed which could add to the number of tricks, barring a dummy reversal). Second, if the same number of tricks are to be made in spades and in notrump, we get a better board for notrump. Choosing notrump was apparently the right decision, although we would have received a bad board with a heart lead.

B. The play:

Of the seven pairs North-South, two played it in spades. Of the five that played it in notrump, one played it from the South side, got a heart lead and was held to four, for a bottom. Of the four who played it from the North side, two made five and two made six. Those who made five, it seems, were unlikely to have received a heart lead, which would have held it to a four (a heart, five spades, and four diamonds). Then they would have to give up control and lose a club and two hearts. They therefore misplayed the hand. They probably (I'm guessing) got a club lead, cashed their spades, returned to hand with a diamond, and could not get back to dummy to cash the jack of diamonds. The key is to first play off the high diamonds. Then, when entering dummy with a spade, cash the jack. Note that if LHO had had hearts instead of RHO, and had led them, we would probably have been held to four for a bottom.

Lessons:

1. Both bidding and play made a difference on this hand.

2. When the "short hand" is balanced, with stops in the off suits, play notrump. An extra ten points might be available and only nine tricks are needed for game.

3. Before playing to trick one, plan the play of the hand, including transportation.

6. A Fix

We face the same two women on this round that we faced on board 5. At the beginning of board 5 I commented about their unpredictability and about how many times I had been fixed by them. On board 5 they had no control. This time they do.

I. What Happened:

A. The bidding:

After a pass by East, partner opened with 1H. West overcalls 1S. I look at my collection:

<pre>
            North
          ♠ 8 6 3 2
          ♥ K 2
          ♦ K Q 7 6 4
          ♣ 10 6
</pre>

What should I do? I felt my choices were 1NT, 2H, 2D, negative double, or pass. I chose 2D. Partner bids 2H after a pass by my LHO. West bids 3C which I pass and LHO bids 3S which buys the contract.

The Bidding

N	E	S	W
	pass	1H	1S
2D	pass	2H	3C
pass	3S	all pass	

B. The play:

I'm on lead and play the king of hearts, which holds, all following. The dummy has this hand:

North
♠ 8 6 3 2
♥ K 2
♦ K Q 7 6 4
♣ 10 6

East (dummy)
♠ 10 7 5
♥ Q 7 4
♦ 5 3 2
♣ A J 9 8

I continue with the two of hearts to partner's jack, declarer following. Partner plays the ace of hearts which is ruffed with the 4S by declarer and overruffed with my

6. I then play the king of diamonds which holds, partner playing the nine. I return the seven of diamonds to partner's ace. The jack of diamonds is ruffed with the nine of spades. Declarer then plays the ace and king of spades, all following; then a club to the ace and the ten of spades from dummy to draw my last trump. Her clubs are then good, for down one.

C. Results:

Tonight we had seven tables, for a top of six. We got a one for our efforts.

North-South Pair Number	Contract	Made	Down	North-South Points	North-South Matchpoints
1.	2HS	3		+140	4
2.	3HS	3		+140	4
3.	3HS		1	-50	0
4.	3HS	5		+200	6
5. (us)	3SW		1	+100	1
6.	3DN	3		+110	2
7.	3HS	3		+140	4

The hands are then exposed:

North (me)
♠ 8 6 3 2
♥ K 2
♦ K Q 7 6 4
♣ 10 6

West
♠ A K 9 4
♥ 8 5
♦ 10 8
♣ K Q 5 4 3

East
♠ 10 7 5
♥ Q 7 4
♦ 5 3 2
♣ A J 9 8

South (partner)
♠ Q J
♥ A J 10 9 6 3
♦ A J 9
♣ 7 2

Good grief. She strikes again. She had 12 highs, a four card spade suit, a passing partner, a LHO who bid freely on the two level, two worthless doubletons, and comes in freely, vulnerable, on the three level with a second bid to steal our hand. And we didn't even double. Maybe I'll give up bridge.

II. What Should Have Been:

A. The bidding:

Partner's one heart opening is normal. The 1 spade overcall is also, although some might prefer 2 clubs. After the one spade bid, I have choices previously referred to, none of which is perfect for my hand. I lack spade control, so 1NT seems wrong. I lack a third heart, so 2H seems wrong. I lack one point for a free two level bid. And, I have nine points, so "pass" seems nondescriptive. I lack clubs, so a negative double doesn't seem right, either. I pick what I think is the least of evils (nonvulnerable) and bid 2D. All of my points seem to be working. Partner bids 2H (showing six pieces, or perhaps five but lacking another bid and also showing minimum values). The 3C is bid on my right. Now what? I have already overbid. If I bid 3H I can just feel partner going to four, thinking I have heart support and almost twelve points. If I pass we may get a plus by setting 3C. Further, partner may have a club stack or she may support diamonds (which I will convert to hearts). I'll pass and see what she does. LHO, however, doesn't let it get that far (by bidding 3S, which gets passed out). I think the bids made by us are not unreasonable. I do not believe that 3C would have bought it, as I expect partner would have bid 3D and we would have ended up in 3H, had LHO not intervened.

Should we double in that sequence? Can partner? The Q-J of spades appear to be worthless. She has three pieces of my suit, cutting down on their defensive value (and West has shown a two-suited hand). She lacks club control. I don't think she has a double. As for me, I have a working heart and perhaps a diamond trick, but that is it. I can't double. It looks like a real fix to me. Next time she may not be so lucky. A fix is, after all, winning with an anti-percentage play. She found the Q-J of spades doubleton, her partner with the ten of spades, and her partner with seven highs (which she had no right to expect), and her fillers in clubs. We'll get her next time (and with a vengence).

B. The play:

First, let's look at what went on at the other tables. Note that pair 3 went down 1 in 3 hearts. Apparently they played for the drop of the queen of hearts. A heart to the king and back to the ace (the odds favor a finesse). Pair 4 made 5 hearts. They must have been given a diamond or a heart lead. Usually a defender is better off not leading the opponents' suits (though not always).

What about our defense? North could conceivably beat the contract by one more trick by not overruffing the third heart trick. In defense of North (normally a steady defender), he must have felt that West had five spades for her bid. And, if West did have five, not overruffing may have cost the defense a trick and insured the contract. North sees that (if West had five spades) West may make five spades and four-five clubs. An overruff, with two hearts and a diamond, perhaps, holds it to three. If North had known that West had only four spades, the holdup is clearly correct. He didn't know. Certainly the ruffing of the heart by West (rather than the pitch of a losing diamond) indicated the presence of a fifth trump. With only four spades, the correct play by West would have been the pitch so that the trumps in dummy would have acted as a monitor against the heart forcing game. Again, West fixed North by making the incorrect play, which happened to work. That rascal.

Lessons:

1. Getting fixed can remove that loving spirit.

2. The bidding on this hand was more important than the play in terms of determining the matchpoint results.

3. Sometimes, when declarer has only four trumps, the failure to overruff declarer (when the defender who has the four trumps has the opportunity) can help declarer lose control of the hand.

4. In defense, other things being equal, leading our suits works better than leading their suits.

7. Two Over One

Week 7
Board 7
Both vulnerable
South Dealer

One of the things which keeps me involved in, and interested in, bridge is the skill/luck ratio, which tends to be very high compared to most other games. There are other things which interest me, of course; but the idea that, for the most part, my fate depends upon my skill is attractive to me.

In bridge, however, the "quality" of one's opponents affects that ratio, also. When the opposition is inexperienced or is not involved, the mistakes they make, which tend to be more frequent than experts' mistakes, tend to randomly "fix" those playing with them. How well you do may then depend upon whether their mistakes are made at your table or at someone else's. This, therefore, lowers the skill/luck ratio.

With that in mind on this board, we face two gentlemen who lack experience.

I. What Happened:

A. The bidding:

I pick up the following:

North
♠ A Q 7 5
♥ K 7
♦ Q J 7 5
♣ 10 8 7

My partner is the dealer, and she passes. RHO bids one spade, which sends a tingle through me as I try to pass without obvious joy. LHO bids two clubs, partner passes and RHO bids 2NT, where it dies.

The Bidding
N	E	S	W
—	—	pass	1S
pass	2C	pass	2NT
all pass			

B. The play:

Rather than lead dummy's suit or declarer's, I have to pick between hearts and diamonds. I select the diamonds and choose the five. As dummy spreads his hand, he says to his partner: "Sorry, partner, I misbid. I really don't have anything."

North (me)
♠ A Q 7 5
♥ K 7
♦ Q J 7 5
♣ 10 8 7

East (dummy)

♠ 10 9
♥ 8 5 3 2
♦ 10 8
♣ K J 9 6 5

Declarer plays the 10 from dummy, which holds. The nine of spades is led to my queen. I switch to the king of hearts, which holds, and follow with the seven to partner's ace. Jo continues hearts and I pitch the seven of clubs. Declarer leads the six of spades from his hand to the ten, which wins the trick. Back comes the eight of diamonds to his hand, followed by the king of spades, which I win. I switch to the eight of clubs to the king and ace. Partner cashes the queen of clubs for down one.

C. Results:

We had eight full tables tonight, for a top of seven. We ended up with a 5½, which isn't bad, though my ego isn't bolstered by it. They happened to make the bidding error at our table, and we did nothing praiseworthy.

North-South Pair Number	Contract	Made	Down	North-South Points	North-South Matchpoints
1.	1SW		1	+100	5½
2.	1SW	1		-80	1½
3.	2NTN		2	-200	0
4.	1SW	1		-80	1½
5. (us)	2NTW		1	+100	5½
6.	2CS	2		+90	3½
7.	1NTN	1		+90	3½
8.	2SW		2	+200	7

The hands are exposed:

North (me)
♠ A Q 7 5
♥ K 7
♦ Q J 7 5
♣ 10 8 7

West (declarer)
♠ K J 8 6 3
♥ Q J 10 9
♦ A K 9
♣ 4

East (dummy)
♠ 10 9
♥ 8 5 3 2
♦ 10 8
♣ K J 9 6 5

South (partner)
♠ 4 2
♥ A 6 4
♦ 6 4 3 2
♣ A Q 3 2

East gave a two over one response with four highs. That's interesting.

II. What Should Have Been:

A. The bidding:

If East had not bid (passed), should South let West buy it at one spade? Of the three who let West buy it, two got a 1½ matchpoint result (by letting them make it) and one set it one trick for a 5½ matchpoint result. It seems the declarer must lose two hearts, a club, two spades and

53

a heart ruff for making one. If South decides to double for takeout, North might bid 1NT, which stands to make. Letting them play one spade unimpeded, though, seems like losing strategy in the long run, as North and South may have half of the points (in this case 22), and perhaps a suit of their own.

B. The play:

The only question which might arise as to the play of the hand has to do with the opening lead. From a three card sequence, the top card is usually led. From a two card sequence, in a notrump contract, most usually lead small (fourth best). There may be some disagreement about this. If South had had a top honor or the 10, the lead of a low card would have been the winning play. As it turns out, it cost the defense a trick.

Lessons:

1. Don't let the opponents buy the contract with a "one of a suit" bid, unless you happen to have a stack in their suit, and don't want them to run.

2. If they fail to do it voluntarily, give weak players every opportunity to overbid or misbid by forcing them a little higher.

3. Bidding was the most important factor on this hand.

8. Low Level Double

Week 8
Board 8
None vulnerable
West Dealer

This week we face two men, one of whom is an old friend (he is sitting East as he did on hands 1 and 2), but this week with a new partner. The new fellow has never played with us before, is quite sharp, and indicates he would like to continue playing each week. That's positive.

I. What Happened:

A. The bidding:

As North I sort the following:

♠ Q J 3
♥ A 7 4
♦ 5 3 2
♣ K 7 5 2

My right hand opponent is the dealer and he passes. I have no bid and neither does LHO. Partner bids one diamond. RHO overcalls one spade. I bid 1NT. East comes in free with two clubs. Partner passes and RHO bids two hearts, which is passed around to partner's double. West decides to rescue himself and bids two spades, which I double. They are playing two spades, doubled.

The Bidding

N	E	S	W
			pass
pass	pass	1D	1S
1NT	2C	pass	2H
pass	pass	double	2S
double	all pass		

B. The play:

What I don't want is for dummy to ruff out the heart losers of declarer and for a cross ruff to start. It appears as though we have the balance of points, with both of their suits stopped. We need, therefore, to get rid of their trumps. I choose the lead of the queen of spades.

North (me)
♠ Q J 3
♥ A 7 4
♦ 5 3 2
♣ K 7 5 2

East (dummy)
♠ 7 6
♥ J 10
♦ J 9 8 6
♣ A 10 8 6 4

East did it again. A free two level bid with six highs. It looks like declarer is in trouble. The queen of spades rides to declarer's king. He leads the nine of clubs to dummy's ace, after some hesitation. This marks him with another club, or two. The jack of hearts rides to my ace. I cash the king of clubs, all following. I then switch to the five of diamonds, won by partner with the king. She cashes the ace of spades followed by the ace of diamonds, declarer dropping the queen. She then leads the queen of hearts to declarer's king. The ten of spades is won by my jack. I return to partner's good nine of hearts with my seven, making declarer's hand good, for down two doubled. We get a +300, which should be a top. It seems like we can't make a game anywhere.

The hands are exposed:

North (me)
- ♠ Q J 3
- ♥ A 7 4
- ♦ 5 3 2
- ♣ K 7 5 2

West (declarer)
- ♠ K 10 9 5 2
- ♥ K 8 3 2
- ♦ Q 7
- ♣ J 9

East (dummy)
- ♠ 7 6
- ♥ J 10
- ♦ J 9 8 6
- ♣ A 10 8 6 4

South (partner)
- ♠ A 8 4
- ♥ Q 9 6 5
- ♦ A K 10 4
- ♣ Q 3

C. Results:

North-South Pair Number	Contract	Made	Down	North-South Points	North-South Matchpoints
1.	1NTN	1		+ 90	1½
2.	1NTN	2		+ 120	4½
3.	1NTN	2		+ 120	4½
4.	4HS		3	-150	0
5. (us)	2SW*		2	+ 300	7
6.	1NTN	3		+ 150	6
7.	2DS	2		+ 90	1½
8.	2SW		2	+ 100	3

As expected, we get a seven on a top of seven. West had little choice after the two club bid but to show his hearts and then to run back to spades. East had no business bidding. It is apparent that the final contract had more input as to the matchpointing than did the play of the hand. As a matter of fact, a pattern seems to be emerging. On all eight hands so far, the bidding had more influence than the play in terms of how well we did. In this case, for the four pairs who played 1NT, making two was about average. Defense and declarer play made some difference here. But for the other four tables, the story was bidding . . . . In our case, it was our opponents' misbids and our willingness to double.

II. What Should Have Happened:

A. The bidding:

East should have taken some bidding lessons. But, apparently he spent his money elsewhere, so let's deal with the situation as North and South found it. After South opens one diamond and West overcalls one spade and North bids one NT, South knows that North and South have more high card points than East and West. North promises at least six for his bid (and South has 15 highs) and probably a ceiling of nine. South therefore knows that North-South have 21-24 high card points between them. Actually North had 10, but he discounted the jack of spades because only one of his spade honors would survive given the expected ace and king in the West hand.

South then is confronted with a two club bid. She should devalue her hand due to the wasted queen of clubs, so she correctly passes. When West bids hearts, the auction takes on new meaning to her. She senses a misfit, has both hearts and spades stopped, has a partner who has shown some points with spades stopped and a probable heart stopper, and realizes that we have more points than they. She doubles correctly. A fine double. When the double is pulled to spades, North doubles. He knows partner has a good hand, and knows that East and West are both passed hands and have a misfit. The golden ace of hearts gives him hope of beating it two tricks. Furthermore, he has nowhere to run, although 2NT is possible (though that would be a rebid of the same values). With neither side vulnerable, to get a good board North and South would have to set an overbid by East-West two tricks doubled to compensate for a partial or part score which they could make.

B. The play:

Nothing out of the ordinary happened. Clearly, the lead of a trump helped the defense. When declarer is two suited, and the defenders have one of the two suits stopped well, and dummy is weak, the lead of trumps usually works.

One misplay by North had no effect, but could have

been costly. When leading his partner's suit (diamonds), he had to select from the five, the three or the two. He picked the five. On the second diamond he had to play the three, as declarer pitched the queen. Now the dummy's jack was high. If Jo Ann played me for a doubleton, she may have led it one more time for me to ruff, giving declarer a pitch on the jack of diamonds. She didn't do that, instead making the fine return of the queen of hearts — almost a costly error. From three small, when leading partner's suit, MUD should be preferred (middle, up, and down). In this case 3-5-2. (This would be consistent with the lead in hand 2.)

Lessons:

1. When your side (defenders) has the balance of power and have the second suit of declarer well stopped, and dummy is weak, leading a trump is a good idea.

2. Trust your partner to have the points they promise you. Assume it is the opponents who are not being accurate.

3. It is not a bad idea to double low level bids (two and three level) if your side has the balance of points, a misfit (or even distribution), and have well placed strength in the opponents' suits.

9. Marginal Slam

Week 9
Board 9
East-West vulnerable
North Dealer

This week is right before Thanksgiving, so we have a small crowd tonight. We have a nine pair Howell movement. Sitting North and South, we face a married couple who normally sit North and South. She, the resident life master at our club and former partner to some of the world's best women players, is sitting East. Her husband is West.

As North I pick up this hand:

North (me)
♠ A 10 6 3
♥ A 5 4 2
♦ 9 5
♣ A K 6

I. What Happened:

A. The bidding:

I opened the bidding with one club. Partner bids one spade. I bid three spades. Partner then bids 4NT. (We play a form of Roman progressive blackwood. Five clubs would mean zero or three aces, five diamonds one or four aces, five hearts means two aces of the same color and five spades means two aces of different color.) I respond five clubs. Partner then bids six spades, our opponents passing throughout.

The Bidding

N	E	S	W
1C	pass	1S	pass
3S	pass	4NT	pass
5C	pass	6S	all pass

B. The play:

Partner is playing the hand. To allow the reader to follow the play, I'll expose both dummy's and declarer's hand.

North (dummy - me)

♠ A 10 6 3
♥ A 5 4 2
♦ 9 5
♣ A K 6

South (partner - declarer)

♠ K Q J 8 4
♥ Q J 9 8
♦ A 3
♣ J 3

The seven of diamonds lead goes to the queen and ace. Partner then plays the king of spades, all following. The queen of spades draws the rest of the trumps. The three of clubs to the ace. The king of clubs and a club ruff eliminates the clubs. Partner exists with a diamond, which is won by LHO with the eight. She needs the rest of the tricks. Back comes the eight of hearts which she wins with the jack. At this point, partner visably flushes. She gets that very sick, rattled look that only comes from having done something one shouldn't do. She goofed and I knew it just by looking at her. She explained, following the hand, that she drew the wrong card from her hand. She meant to play the nine. The queen of hearts is covered by the king and ace. She then loses the nine of hearts to the ten and is down one.

The hands are then exposed:

North (me)
- ♠ A 10 6 3
- ♥ A 5 4 2
- ♦ 9 5
- ♣ A K 6

West
- ♠ 5 2
- ♥ K 10 8
- ♦ K J 8 7
- ♣ Q 7 5 2

East
- ♠ 9 7
- ♥ 7 3
- ♦ Q 10 6 4 2
- ♣ 10 9 8 4

South (declarer)
- ♠ K Q J 8 4
- ♥ Q J 9 6
- ♦ A 3
- ♣ J 3

C. Results:

One embarrassed partner ("We shouldn't include this hand."). Aside from personal discomfort, here is what happened:

North-South Pair Number	Contract	Made	Down	North-South Points	North-South Matchpoints
3.	6NTS	6		+990	3
5.	6NTS		1	-50	0
6.	4NTS	5		+450	1½
8.	4NTS	5		+450	1½

We got a bottom. It appears that only five can be made on the hand. Pair number three must have received some help.

II. What Should Have Been:

A. The bidding:

Jo Ann and I play what is called a "variable notrump." That means that when we are vulnerable our notrump range is 15-17. Not vulnerable it is 12-14. Therefore, opening 1NT was not possible on this hand. Some who play a conventional notrump may have elected to do that.

The question about the bidding then has to do with North's jump to three spades and South's push to slam.

North shows 16-18 points with four card support for spades for his bid. He has 15 highs and a doubleton. All 15 points are "working." I believe he falls squarely in the middle of this range.

South has 14 highs and 2 doubletons (one of the points in the doubleton may be wasted). Let's give South, in terms of evaluation, about 15-16 points. However, the combined total, from South's point of view is therefore

31-34 points, with 33 needed for slam. I would term this a marginal slam. What of the value of South's points? Six of the points are in the spade suit and four of the points are in queens and jacks. No runable suit. Two doubletons. I would call the slam, from South's point of view, "low marginal." As we see from the results, six spades does not make given average defense. And, playing the field we confront on the local level, pushing to a marginal slam is poor business. If she happened to make six anyhow (on a bid of four spades), she would have a good board. Why risk a bid of six when most of the field is in four and you have a marginal slam? We noticed on hand 3 that pushing for a marginal game was also counterproductive.

B. The play:

After the diamond lead (which doesn't help things), it is apparent that either she gets a diamond pitch somewhere or has to find the king of hearts onside with a certain heart split, or must get a heart lead from LHO. Jo Ann tried for a ruff and a slough. That would not have helped her at all. She had no choice but to lead the queen of hearts and to hope it was covered. She then had to hope the ten of hearts was doubleton or could be finessed coming back. In the actual case, she got lucky in that West did lead a heart and that East did not overtake the eight of diamonds and push back a heart or diamond, and also lucky that West did not, instead of returning a heart, return a diamond or club. However, as the cards lie, making five is the limit.

Lessons:

1. Pushing to marginal slams is poor policy on the local level.

2. Bidding is again very important in terms of determining matchpoint allocation.

3. Side suits in trump contracts may determine the success of the slam. It is not enough (in terms of hand evaluation) to have strength in the trump suit.

10. Let Them Play The Misfits

Week 10
Board 10
Both vulnerable
East Dealer

Again we have a Howell movement with 11 pairs this time. We are sitting opposite a pair of gentlemen we encountered on hand 3. At that time the East-West interference and input was minimal. We had total control. This time there is a difference. The pair we face has some unusual bids which periodically require inquiry. Their system changes so often that the opponents (and perhaps themselves) are never sure of the meaning of their bids.

I. What Happened:

A. The bidding:

As North I pick up these cards:

North (me)
♠ 9 8 2
♥ A K 9 6 4
♦ J 10 9
♣ Q 3

Ten highs and a five card major. LHO is dealer and he bids one heart. Looks like someone is about to find a misfit. Partner passes and RHO bids 1NT. I pass and LHO ventures two spades, which is passed around to me. I ask RHO the meaning of the bid and he says, "Either he has 18 or 19 points or has a hand unsuited for no trump." That tells me that RHO likes spades better than hearts, of course, and that he must be weak. Therefore, partner must have (giving RHO about six points . . . which is what would pass a possible 19 and still find a 1NT response) 5-11 points — perhaps about eight, the average. I have no reason to expect that we have a fit, I sense a mismatch, and we are vulnerable. Furthermore, queens and jacks are better for defense. I pass.

The Bidding

N	E	S	W
	1H	pass	1NT
pass	2S	all pass	

B. The play:

Partner leads the queen of diamonds and dummy is spread.

North (me)
♠ 9 8 2
♥ A K 9 6 4
♦ J 10 9
♣ Q 3

West (dummy)

♠ 7 4 3

♥ J

♦ 8 5 4 2

♣ A J 7 4 2

Partner must have either a singleton queen or a doubleton queen. She would have led queen only from that or queen-jack. (We lead king from king-queen.) I play the nine and declarer wins. A small heart goes to partner's queen. Back comes another diamond to declarer's other honor. A low heart is ruffed in dummy. Declarer cashes dummy's ace of clubs on which he pitches a diamond. A club ruff in his hand is followed by another low heart which partner ruffs with the ten and dummy pitches a diamond. Partner then leads a spade to declarer's ace. Another heart lead is ruffed by partner's jack. Partner leads a club which is ruffed with declarer's king. Declarer leads the six of diamonds which is ruffed by dummy's seven and overruffed with my eight. I cash the ace of hearts and then yield the last trick to declarer's ten of hearts, making two.

The hands are spread:

North (me)
♠ 9 8 2
♥ A K 9 6 4
♦ J 10 9
♣ Q 3

West (dummy)
♠ 7 4 3
♥ J
♦ 8 5 4 2
♣ A J 7 4 2

East (declarer)
♠ A K Q 5
♥ 10 8 7 5 3
♦ A K 7 6
♣

South (partner)
♠ J 10 6
♥ Q 2
♦ Q 3
♣ K 10 9 8 6 5

Jo Ann had her eight points, as I expected.

C. Results:

North-South Pair Number	Contract	Made	Down	North-South Points	North-South Matchpoints
1.	2HN*			-800	½
2.	1HE	1		-80	4
3. (us)	2SE	2		-110	3
4.	2HN*		2	-500	2
5.	2CS*		3	-800	½

We got a three on a top of four. It is obvious that the

final contract determined, in large part, how many match-points you got. Bidding is important.

II. What Should Have Been:

A. The bidding:

We are concerned with North and South bidding, of course. Both North and South did well to stay out of the auction instead of bidding to balance. South would have had to go to 3C, which would have been dangerous, and South knows there is a misfit. Better to let them play the hands which are misfits, especially when you don't have a very strong suit, or a reason to expect that you and your partner have a joint suit. Just choosing to play defense will get one a decent board when misfits happen.

B. The play:

As we have already mentioned, the bidding was the main thing. But, let's take a look at the play to see if anything significant happened. First of all, what may happen on a particular hand may be an aberration in terms of playing the percentages. Perhaps this hand illustrates that fact.

Jo Ann selected the lead of the queen of diamonds from queen small. Most experts (Blackwood, for example) would say that this is a bad lead. Let's look at her choices and what she knows from the bidding. She knows that East has at least five hearts and probably four spades. She knows that, because she has two hearts and West did not support hearts, West lacks three hearts. She assumes that West would have bid one spade over one heart if he had four and if he had a weak hand. Therefore, South should know that East-West have at most seven spades between them (probably a 4-3 fit). She also may guess that if West had two hearts he may have (perhaps a small percentage of the time), with a weak hand, passed one heart. West may have, therefore, three spades (or perhaps two) with one or two hearts (perhaps one). Therefore, it would follow that East will ruff the hearts in dummy. (South's partner is marked for four or five). From the look of South's clubs, South must assume a cross-ruff will be attempted by declarer. Where are North's points? South assumes they are in diamonds. If they are, given bad splits in the other suits, they will always be of value. Furthermore, the name of the game when declarer has a 4-3 fit is to try the forcing game. Given the absence of knowledge of North's long suit (if he has one other than hearts), leading trumps would be a safe lead. South knows that hearts are not splitting for declarer, so she will, if East tries to ruff one following a spade lead, always get her ruff in if she wants it.

Then, when declarer leads small toward the jack, and she wins the queen, she knows North has an honor in hearts and has probably five. She should then return a spade.

On this hand, the above strategy may not work. Double dummy, given an underlead of the queen of clubs later in the play, a club forcing game may work. But normally, a trump lead is best, I feel.

Lessons:

1. When declarer and dummy have a misfit, and points are fairly evenly distributed, leading trump will tend to be positive.

2. Balancing when the hands are a misfit is negative. If they have a misfit, you probably do also.

3. Thinking of declarer's likely mode of attack often leads to the best defense. Normally, do that which you can to counter that likely mode of attack.

11. Play For A Plus

Week 11
Board 11
No one vulnerable
South Dealer

This week we have 6½ tables, which ordinarily means a Mitchell movement. Our director elected to have a 13 pair Howell movement instead. We face two women who normally sit North-South and are among the least experienced North-South players at our club.

As North I pick up another exciting hand:

North (me)
♠ A Q 9 3
♥ 6 5 4
♦ Q 9 8 7
♣ 9 7

I. What Happened:

A. The bidding:

Partner passed as did RHO. I have no bid, so I pass. LHO bids one diamond. Partner doubles (I assume she has 10-12 points and support for the unbid suits, especially the majors), RHO passes again and I bid one spade. LHO bids two diamonds, which is passed around to me. I decide to pass, for reasons to be dealt with later.

The Bidding

N	E	S	W
—	—	pass	pass
pass	1D	double	pass
1S	2D	all pass	

B. The play:

Partner leads the eight of spades and dummy is exposed:

North (me)
♠ A Q 9 3
♥ 6 5 4
♦ Q 9 8 7
♣ 9 7

West (dummy)
♠ K J
♥ K J 7 3
♦ 5 3
♣ J 10 6 4 2

Dummy had nine highs and failed to find a bid. Between dummy and myself we have 17 highs. That leaves only 23. If partner has 10-12, declarer must be a bit weak in high cards. In any event, the jack is played from dummy and I take my queen. I switch to the nine of clubs which is taken by partner with the ace, declarer first playing the king. Partner returns the five of clubs which rides to declarer's queen. A heart is led to partner's ace. Back comes the eight of clubs for me to ruff, which I do. I play the ace of spades, followed by the nine which is taken by declarer's ten. The queen of hearts is overtaken and a diamond returned to declarer's ten and partner's king. Partner returns the ten of hearts to dummy's jack and declarer ruffs with the four. The ace of diamonds folowed by a diamond to my queen ends the damage. Down 2 gives us a plus 100.

The hands are exposed:

North (me)
♠ A Q 9 3
♥ 6 5 4
♦ Q 9 8 7
♣ 9 7

West (dummy)
♠ K J
♥ K J 7 3
♦ 5 3
♣ J 10 6 4 2

East (declarer)
♠ 10 6 2
♥ Q 2
♦ A J 10 6 4
♣ K Q 3

South (partner)
♠ 8 7 5 4
♥ A 10 9 8
♦ K 2
♣ A 8 5

North-South have 21 highs and East-West have 19. Another battle in the trenches. It seems as though this is where games are won or lost.

Making that progressive squeeze to bring in the grand slam makes good reading, but rarely occurs. We much more frequently see partials with points evenly distributed between the two sides. It is therefore much more important.

C. Results:

It looks like two spades makes. In any event, we played it "safe" and got a 3½ on a top of five. (The pair numbers below are "compressed" to simplify reading.)

North-South Pair Number	Contract	Made	Down	North-South Points	North-South Matchpoints
1. (us)	2DE		2	+100	3½
2.	2SN	2		+110	5
3.	2NTW		1	+50	2
4.	3CW	3		-110	0
5.	2DE		2	+100	3½
6.	passed out			—	1

How in the world three clubs makes is a mystery (unless the ace of spades is led).

II. What Should Have Been:

A. The bidding:

I was not meaning to bore my readers, but the bidding was again central. Honestly, when I began this project I had no idea that bidding was so much more important than the play, but that is the way it appears. I guess the reason I thought both were about equal (or even that play and defense were more important) was the weight given to play in other literature. Few books deal with bidding strategy.

On this hand, which is perhaps typical in some ways, North-South have choices to make. North and South should certainly pass the first round. Then, when West bids one diamond, South's double is very descriptive. North, knowing that South is a passed hand, should bid only one spade. When two diamonds is bid by North's LHO, and it gets passed around to North, he has a problem. Should he bid two spades or pass; North has no support for South in clubs or hearts. He has two wasted points in diamonds, and poor distribution. Furthermore, he knows that (assuming South has about 11 points) North and South have 19 points or so (two of which are wasted on offense). We could easily get a minus with 17 working points. Furthermore, the diamonds look good for defense. The queen is not wasted there. And, with a weak dummy, declarer will have to play it out of his hand. Play for a plus. East and West do not apparently have a fit. In hands where the points are evenly distributed, playing for a plus is important.

Let's look for a moment at East and West and their bidding. East has a tough time justifying a second bid, though she knows that North and South are both passed hands. West missed the boat by not bidding two clubs over the double (that would show less than ten points).

One further point needs to be made. East, after three passes, has the option of passing the hand out. East has a marginal bid in terms of point count (twelve highs). Further, she has no control over the majors. In fact, she is very weak in the majors. If she had passed out the hand, they would have done much better. The point is this: In fourth position, after three passes, bid only with a full opener. With a marginal opener, and lacking control in the majors, it is better to pass. If not, you may be outbid at low levels.

In any event, re-evaluating North's hand is the key. It is downgraded on offense and upgraded on defense. North has no reason to expect, furthermore, that the missing cards will be so favorably placed. Two spades could have easily gone down with a less favorable placement of the cards. Play for a plus.

B. The play:

Nothing particularly significant happened in the play of the hand. It is again the bidding to which attention must be paid.

Lessons:

1. If you think that you can set the opponents and points are evenly distributed between both sides, play for a plus and a better than average score. (This presumes the lack of wild distribution.)

2. When trying to decide whether to bid or pass in a situation, re-evaluating one's hand, given what has occurred in the bidding to that point, will often provide the key as to whether one's hand is better suited for offense or defense. Queens in the opponent's trump suit, with length in that suit, are valuable for defense but often worthless for offense.

3. Trust your partner to have the points he/she promises you.

4. In fourth seat (after three passes), with a marginal hand and lacking good major suit holdings (particularly spades), pass.

12. Down The Line

Week 12
Board 12
North-South vulnerable
West Dealer

This week we encounter two women who normally don't play together. We met the East player once before. She sat West on hand 1.

I. What Happened:

A. The bidding:

As North I picked up this hand:

> North
> ♠ K 10 5 3
> ♥ A K Q 9
> ♦ J
> ♣ Q 7 6 5

Fifteen highs and a singleton. Or, better still, in terms of evaluation, 14 highs and a singleton. Jo Ann and I play a Roman two diamond bid. That means that an opening of two diamonds indicates 11-14 highs and 5-4-4 or 4-4-4-1 distribution. My experience has been that when we open two diamonds we do very well on that board, as it is such a specific bid. However, rather than lie to partner (I do have 15 highs), and because she can respond to a one opener in a major if she has one, I choose one club. There is a 1D overcall to my left, and partner bids 1H. I jump to three and all pass.

The Bidding

N	E	S	W
—	—	—	pass
1C	1D	1H	pass
3H	all pass		

B. The play:

My RHO leads the king of diamonds. For the sake of readability, let's look at the play from Jo Ann's standpoint.

North (dummy - me)

♠ K 10 5 3
♥ A K Q 9
♦ J
♣ Q 7 6 5

South (Jo Ann)

♠ J 7 6 2
♥ J 5 4 2
♦ A 9 4 3
♣ 9

Partner takes the king of diamonds with her ace. Now how would you play the hand? Cross-ruff or draw trumps and hope the ace-queen of spades are not on your right? Jo Ann picked the cross ruff. She led the nine of clubs from hand at trick two, taken by the ace on her right, as LHO failed to cover. RHO returned the queen of diamonds which is ruffed by dummy. She then ruffs a club, and leads another diamond. LHO pitches a spade and she ruffs in dummy. Another club ruff to her hand and another diamond ruff in dummy (LHO pitches the king of clubs). The queen of clubs from dummy is ruffed with her jack of hearts. Then the 2 of spades to the 9-10 and ace. The seven of hearts returns to dummy's ace. The king of spades is ruffed by RHO and she ends up down 1 for a minus 100.

C. Results:

Take a guess. How do you think we did going down one in three hearts? Would you believe a tie for bottom?

North-South Pair Number	Contract	Made	Down	North-South Points	North-South Matchpoints
1.	4SS	4		+ 620	5½
2.	4SS	4		+ 620	5½
3.	2SS	3		+ 140	4
4.	4HS		1	-100	1½
5. (us)	3HS		1	-100	1½
6.	3HS		1	-100	1½
7.	3HS		1	-100	1½

The winning contract was spades, not hearts. Surprise! The hands are then exposed:

North (dummy)

♠ K 10 5 3

♥ A K Q 9

♦ J

♣ Q 7 6 5

West

♠ Q 9 8 4

♥ 10 6 3

♦ K 2

♣ K J 10 2

East

♠ A

♥ 8 7

♦ Q 10 8 7 6 5

♣ A 8 4 3

South (Jo Ann)

♠ J 7 6 2

♥ J 5 4 2

♦ A 9 4 3

♣ 9

II. What Should Have Been:

A. The bidding:

I see nothing wrong with the way we bid the hand. If Jo Ann were to have responded with spades first, she would not have found a heart fit if North lacked spades. Most experts, I believe, would have bid the hearts with her hand. Suppose North had bid 1NT in response to 1 spade. She could not have said 2 hearts, and would miss that critical 4-4 fit. North-South pairs 1-3 got lucky, in my opinion. Or, phrased differently, we got fixed. Bidding your majors up the line, particularly with weak hands (where you may not have a second bid) is the thing to do.

B. The play:

Jo Ann needs nine tricks. From looking at the hand, she must believe that any pair who bid game is doomed, with normal breaks. Therefore, just making three should be a good board. Where can she see nine tricks? With luck, the ace of diamonds and three diamond ruffs, three club ruffs and the jack of hearts, together falling with the ace of hearts, makes eight. She needs to make a spade trick. What happened is that her spade got ruffed.

By not cross-ruffing, she could have, assuming a 3-2 break in hearts, counted, with luck, 3 spade tricks, 4 hearts, a diamond and 3 club ruffs (at best). At worst she would have two spade tricks, four hearts, a diamond and two club ruffs. She would take, therefore, 9-11 tricks. She only took eight as she played it. It might be played by, at trick two, leading a spade to the ten. When the queen of diamonds is returned, pitch a spade (or club) from the board. Then, if East continues with the ten of diamonds, ruff high (your nine of diamonds is now set up), and lead a small club from the board. Now you have them. If East wins with the ace, he can do no better than return a diamond which has the effect of drawing West's trump (if he ruffs), and you overruff. In any event, you will make your nine tricks. At worst you will lose a club, a diamond, a spade and a spade ruff.

The problem came from ruffing diamonds in dummy. You gain nothing by doing that. Just ruffing clubs in the closed hand gets you the extra necessary tricks.

I should note that following the hand, I felt a cross-ruff was best. After studying the hand, I changed my mind. In the heat of battle one does not have much time to study the hand.

Lessons:

1. When playing in a partial, it is important to get a plus score.

2. The correct bidding procedure is not going to work on all hands, but will work on more hands than incorrect bidding procedures. Play the percentages.

3. With weak hands, bid your majors up the line.

13. Think Conservative

Week 13
Board 13
Both vulnerable
North Dealer

Two women face us this week, one of whom we have seen before. The woman sitting East sat West on board 11. So what?

Jo Ann and I have been playing well tonight. Except for one major error on defense which I made (which I am not obliged to tell you about, incidently), we have made very few errors. This is the last round of the evening, and we feel as though we have a lock on first place tonight. (It later turns out that despite being 2½ boards over average, we came in second.) So, I'm in a pretty good mood. As I look at the following hand, my mind flashes back to my defensive error.

```
          North
     ♠  8 7 4 3
     ♥  6 2
     ♦  6 2
     ♣  Q 10 4 3 2
```

Nothing to take my mind off of my blunder.

By the way, are you getting a little tired of these weak hands? Believe it or not, for the first 13 boards I had an average of 9.92 points/hand and Jo Ann had an average of 11.23. Average is 10.00, of course. Apparently our hands are fairly representative.

I. What Happened:

A. The bidding:

I pass, of course. LHO bids one club, Jo says one diamond, RHO says one heart, and I pass again. LHO says two hearts and RHO jumps to four. Then all pass.

	The Bidding		
N	E	S	W
pass	1C	1D	1H
pass	2H	pass	4H
	all pass		

B. The play:

I'm on lead and pick the six of diamonds (partner's suit) from my holding of two diamonds (6 and 2). Dummy comes down with the following:

East (dummy)
♠ A Q 9
♥ 10 9 7 3
♦ A 10 3
♣ K 8 5

Nothing unusual in terms of her bidding. The ace is played from dummy. Declarer then draws trumps in two rounds, all following. She next plays three winning rounds of spades (won by ace, king and queen). I have the case spade. Then a club to her ace and a club back to her king, and she exits with a diamond to her jack and Jo Ann's king. Partner attempts to cash the queen of diamonds which is ruffed, and declarer gives up a club to my queen after leading out her trumps, making five. We get a minus 650.

Take a guess. First let me show you the hands.

North (me)
♠ 8 7 4 3
♥ 6 2
♦ 6 2
♣ Q 10 4 3 2

West (declarer)
♠ K 10 5
♥ A K Q 8 5
♦ J 9
♣ A 9 7

East (dummy)
♠ A Q 9
♥ 10 9 7 3
♦ A 10 3
♣ K 8 5

South (Jo Ann)
♠ J 6 2
♥ J 4
♦ K Q 8 7 5 4
♣ J 6

We get a 2½ on an average of 3. Below average.

North-South Pair Number	Contract	Made	Down	North-South Points	North-South Matchpoints
1.	6HW		1	+100	5½
2.	6HE	6		-1430	0
3.	4HW	5		-650	2½
4.	6HW		1	+100	5½
5. (us)	4HW	5		-650	2½
6.	4HW	5		-650	2½
7.	4HW	5		-650	2½

They never seem to push for slam at our table.

II. What Should Have Been:

A. The bidding:

East-West have 30 HCPs between them. They have no outstanding distributional features. East bid her hand as if she had 13-15 points, which she did. West, with 17 highs and relative balance, knows that slam is marginal at best. She makes the right play and stops in game (and is rewarded with an above average board).

B. The play:

Declarer must lose a diamond and a club (when North is on lead). The only hope is for the winner of the diamond trick to mysteriously try to cash the long spade. Barring that, she has no play for six.

At one table six was made, however, and from the East side. East's opening of one heart is strange, but it worked this time. South may have opened with the king of diamonds. Then, after drawing trumps, declarer may have led a small diamond to dummy's jack. South would win with the queen, but declarer's ten would enable declarer to pitch a club from dummy for making six.

Lessons:

1. Again, the overriding lesson with marginal hands is don't go for slam (note board nine).

2. With marginal hands lacking outstanding distribution of features, be especially conservative.

14. Decisions

Tonight we have 5½ tables and this is our last round. We have just finished four boards with two women who gave us three bottoms . . . we had no control over the hands. Right now we're pretty irritated, and Jo is not feeling 100%.

We face two gentlemen tonight.

I. What Happened:

A. The bidding:

I pick up a five-five hand with six highs.

```
        North
   ♠ 10
   ♥ 9 7
   ♦ J 10 8 5 3
   ♣ A J 10 6 5
```

Partner opens the bidding with one spade after a pass by her RHO. My RHO doubles and puts me under the gun. We play that a redouble shows 10 + points with no fit. A jump to 2NT shows 10-12 points with a fit, and a jump to 3NT shows 13-15 points with a fit. Any other bid means less than 10 points. I decide to step in and muddy the waters (I sense a heart fit for them), so I bid two diamonds. I will still be able to bid again without misleading partner about the strength of my hand. LHO bids two hearts. Partner bids two spades. RHO bids 2NT and again I am under the gun. Should I bid three clubs? Should I pass and conceal my clubs? Should I bid clubs for a lead if they play in hearts? Tough decision. I pass. LHO bids three hearts (as expected) and RHO goes back to 3NT, which is passed out.

The Bidding

N	E	S	W
	pass	1S	double
2D	2H	2S	2NT
pass	3H	pass	3NT
	all pass		

B. The play:

Again I have a tough decision. What do I lead? RHO has implied that he has spades and diamonds well stopped. Hearts is out of the question. I have a concealed club suit five cards long with three honors. If I catch partner with the king of clubs or an early entry and she can push back a club we can set this. That does not seem like too much to ask for. (Perhaps she has a heart stop or a spade). We ought to be able to beat this contract. Jo Ann and I have a system which states that the lead of the "10" indicates

93

(against no trump) that the leader has either 10-9-8 etc. or the "10", the jack and one higher honor but not the queen. With 10-jack-queen, the queen would be led. It looks like a perfect situation for the lead of the ten of clubs.

Dummy is exposed with no surprises:

North (me)
♠ 10
♥ 9 7
♦ J 10 8 5 3
♣ A J 10 6 5

East (dummy)
♠ 2
♥ A K 10 5 4 2
♦ 4 2
♣ 9 8 3 2

Dummy plays low, partner her queen, and declarer his king. The nine in dummy will stop me. Declarer plays his queen of hearts all following. A heart to the king means that six hearts will be cashed. Then, a finesse of the queen of spades holds. Declarer cashes his ace of spades for his ninth trick. He then exits with the seven of diamonds. Partner overtakes my ten with her ace. She cashes the king of spades and exits with a diamond. Declarer's king and queen are good, making five. We are minus 460, which has to be a bottom.

C. Results:

The hands are exposed:

North (me)
♠ 10
♥ 9 7
♦ J 10 8 5 3
♣ A J 10 6 5

West (declarer)
♠ A Q 9 5 4
♥ Q 8
♦ K Q 9 7
♣ K 4

East (dummy)
♠ 2
♥ A K 10 5 4 2
♦ 4 2
♣ 9 8 3 2

South (partner)
♠ K J 8 7 6 3
♥ J 6 3
♦ A 6
♣ Q 7

The bottom we expected is not quite a bottom. Some-one bid three spades with the South hand and got doubl-ed. We managed a one.

North-South Pair Number	Contract	Made	Down	North-South Points	North-South Matchpoints
1.	1SW	1		-80	3
2.	4HE		1	+50	4
3.	3SS*		3	-500	0
4. (us)	3NTW	5		-460	1
5.	2HE	3		-140	2

How is that for some variety? Passed out in one spade? It did not matter if they made five notrump or three in terms of our result (we only had 5½ tables). It would probably have mattered if we had ten tables, as the likelihood of some pairs making four hearts or playing the hand in 3NT would be increased. How they stopped in two hearts is also tough to perceive.

II. What Should Have Been:

A. The bidding:

I think that Jo Ann's hand is too weak to open the bidding. She has 11 highs (two of which are suspect) and ony 1½ quick tricks. Perhaps she comes closer to a weak two spade opener than a one opener in second position. I'd probably pass with her hand. But, to bid twice is wrong, in my opinion. She certainly had nothing extra to show me, and East came in free at the two level after my announced weakness.

If she had not bid, East-West may still have found 3NT, but her bid may have misled partner, which might have been important in other circumstances.

As to North's intervention with "two diamonds" rather than "two clubs" or "pass", if they had ended up in hearts, a diamond lead would have been unfortunate in many circumstances. It is certainly debatable as to whether or not he should intervene. In retrospect, the likelihood of a heart contract, given the bidding and North's shortness, is greater than the likelihood of a notrump contract. Therefore, a club lead would be better and no diamond bid would make that more likely. If, however, North wanted to give South the choice of suits in an attempt to balance a two heart bid, intervening with diamonds first would be necessary. Which is correct is debatable. Given South's opening bid, North assumes that he will have the opportunity to balance, as East-West lack game points.

B. The play:

The only mistakes were made toward the end of the hand. Jo Ann either should have not overtaken my ten of diamonds at trick ten (she had ace small) or overtaken it, cashed her spade, and returned a club. We had the last four tricks. She erred by not remembering that I had the two top clubs left. With the nine of clubs in dummy, she had to know I had the ace and the jack left. She did have a club left when she pushed back a diamond after cashing her king of spades.

Lessons:

1. Opening light may deceive partner.

2. Sometimes, when decisions have to be made, not all of the information is available to make the best decision. Weighing all variables and then making an educated choice is the best that can be done. This often involves predicting the direction the bidding is likely to take.

15. Intervention

Let me explain. We have had a terrible night. Not only are we not communicating, but we are getting our share of fixes. Nothing seems to be going right, and the night is lost in terms of "scratching." Along come the LOL's who are unpredicatble and who give us our share of fixes. I'm in a bad mood and Jo Ann has still not recovered completely from her bout with the flu which she suffered last week. Now that I have paved the way, here is the culmination of our evening.

I. What Happened:

A. The bidding:

As North I pick up a nice hand:

North (me)

♠ 9
♥ K 8 5 4
♦ A K J 8 5
♣ A Q 4

I have 17 highs and a singleton spade. After two passes I make the normal bid of one diamond. Partner says one spade. RHO injects a bid of two hearts. Without much thought I "double", which is passed out.

The Bidding

N	E	S	W
		pass	pass
1D	pass	1S	2H
double	all pass		

B. The play:

Feeling as though we have the balance of high cards, with the off suits stopped, I want to prevent ruffs in dummy, so I lead the four of hearts. Dummy surfaces with probably more than declarer had the right to expect.

North (me)

♠ 9
♥ K 8 5 4
♦ A K J 8 5
♣ A Q 4

East (dummy)

♠ A J 8 6
♥ 6 2
♦ Q 10
♣ 9 8 7 6 3

My four of hearts goes to declarer's queen, partner playing the jack. The queen of spades rides to partner's king. Partner shifts to the seven of hearts, which is won by declarer's nine. A spade continuation is ruffed by me. I play three successful rounds of diamonds, partner discarding on the third. A fourth diamond goes to declarer's nine. Her ace of hearts drops my king. The hand ends uneventfully, making two. We took a spade, a heart and three diamonds. Notice how brief I can make the description to avoid belaboring the embarrassment.

C. Results:

I see no possibility of getting anything but a bottom. The results are in and we are rewarded justly for our bidding and play. Fortunately, a zero is bottom. If they awarded minuses, we would have earned one.

North-South Pair Number	Contract	Made	Down	North-South Points	North-South Matchpoints
1.	3NTN	5		+660	3
2.	2DN		1	-100	1
3.	3NTN	4		+630	2
4.	3NTN	6		+690	4
5. (us)	2HW*	2		-570	0

The hands are exposed with no great surprises:

North (me)
♠ 9
♥ K 8 5 4
♦ A K J 8 5
♣ A Q 4

West (declarer)
♠ Q 4 3 2
♥ A Q 10 9 3
♦ 9 7 4 2
♣

East (dummy)
♠ A J 8 6
♥ 6 2
♦ Q 10
♣ 9 8 7 6 3

South (Jo Ann)
♠ K 10 7 5
♥ J 7
♦ 6 3
♣ K J 10 5 2

North and South have 25 highs between them.

II. What Should Have Been:

A. The bidding:

Obviously, it did not matter if we set the contract one, two, or three tricks. We would have received the same result (a "1"). We got a zero by letting them make it, which is only a "1" point difference. Therefore, it was the bidding which mattered the most. I see no problem with North's opener or South's response of one spade. The problem lies with the "double", obviously. North has a choice. He can double, bid 2NT, bid 3NT, or pass, as I see it. A three diamond call would misrepresent the strength of the hand (I feel that a pass would, also). Rather than take the chance that a 2NT bid would be passed out, the winning call would be 3NT. It is probably better to double than to play in 2NT. But, the question is this: How can north know that 3NT is the winning call? What information does he have?

He knows that South has six or more points. That gives his side from 23 points up. He assumes (perhaps wrongly) that he can count on two clubs, a heart, and five diamonds. If partner has one trick (spades or hearts, for example), he is a lock for nine tricks. His long diamond suit, the fact that the opponents' strength appears to be favorably located, and the fear of missing a vulnerable game should tip his decision in favor of a 3NT bid. Perfection with intervention is difficult to achieve. We have already noted that it is unwise to bid marginal games. However, North does not know that it is marginal. Furthermore, he has other considerations on this hand. The king of hearts can be counted as an ace in trick-taking potential, as the ace is known to be on the right. North should have taken more time and reached the logical conclusion reached by this author.

B. The play:

Both North and South misdefended. The opening heart lead is defensible, even perhaps correct. With the strength concentrated North and South, North doesn't want the high cards ruffed in dummy. When South gets in (following the finesse of the spade), she should switch to clubs. She has to forsee an endplay against North, and the possibility of "forcing" declarer.

North, for his part, should not have trumped the second spade. He is giving declarer a "loser on loser" play (his king of hearts drops after he ruffs once). Declarer pitches his automatic loser in spades. If North does not ruff, but rather pitches, he gets his heart anyhow, and South gets her spade. Where can declarer then go? Furthermore, North should not have cashed the jack of diamonds, as declarer is then endplayed in diamonds. In summary, the contract should have been set from 2 to 3 tricks. Very poor defense. But, it did not matter that much in terms of matchpointing.

Lessons:

1. When your opponents are vulnerable, and you are not, sticking in a two level overcall when they are both bidding may make it more difficult for them to perfectly evaluate the strength of their hands. They may find it hard to know if they belong in game or not. It has great preemptive value.

2. Point count and that "magic 26" sometimes are less important than where the cards lie and long runable suits.

3. Doubling (for penalty) low level non-vulnerable overcalls when you are vulnerable and have "marginal or better" game strength tends to be losing strategy.

4. Not letting poor results on previous hands in an evening influence the hand you're playing will tend to (overall) increase your scores for a given evening. Play one hand at a time.

16. Weak Notrumps

Week 16
Board 16
East-West vulnerable
West Dealer

This week we're playing a five table Howell movement with 10 pairs. It is right after the Christmas break, so Jo Ann and I are probably a bit rusty. (How is that for an excuse for what is about to befall me?)

This week we meet the director and his partner. They usually play North-South, but, due to the type of movement, they are sitting East-West on this board. They play Precision (the only ones at the club to do that), but a "loose" Precision. Once a week bridge may not be enough time together to really develop a system and to explore its intricacies.

As North I pick up another average hand:

North
♠ A K
♥ J 9 6 3 2
♦ 8 7
♣ J 9 7 5

Nine highs and two doubletons.

I. What Happened:

A. The bidding:

RHO is the dealer and he opens 1NT (13-15 points). Somehow, when I face a 13-15 or 12-14 NT bid, which is termed "weak", I feel at liberty to jump right in. After all, it is weak. Right? Wrong! That is a misnomer. Why don't we rename that bid to prevent ourselves from overdoing it and from thinking we have all the points. Call it a "low notrump bid" or whatever. But, "weak" is misleading. In any event, I bid two hearts. LHO doubles and all pass. Short and not so sweet.

The Bidding
North

N	E	S	W
			1NT (13-15)
2H	double all pass		

B. The play:

LHO leads the king of diamonds and Jo Ann lays down six highs. I could be in trouble!

North (declarer - me)

♠ A K
♥ J 9 6 3 2
♦ 8 7
♣ J 9 7 5

South (dummy)

♠ 9 5 4 2

♥ 5 4

♦ Q 6 5 4

♣ A 4 2

The king of diamonds lead holds, all following. Glancing at the hand I note that they are vulnerable and have 25 highs. LHO is marked with 11 or 12. If they have a game, we're in good shape. If not, we're still in good shape if noone bid it and I hold it to down one. We're only in bad shape if people bid game and went down and/or some made partials and I go down more than one.

LHO shifts at trick two to the ten of clubs. At this point the reader may want to take stock. How would you play from this point on? Say you let the ten ride, the queen wins on your right. RHO shifts to a spade. Now, what would you do? I won, returned a diamond to the ace of LHO. He shifted to the eight of spades which I won. I then entered dummy with the ace of clubs, RHO dropping the king. A low heart is led from dummy, RHO producing the seven, I duck and LHO wins with the eight. He shifts to clubs to give RHO a ruff. A diamond back to the queen of dummy. A heart lead goes to the ace of RHO. The ten of diamonds is ruffed by me and I give LHO his heart king and then claim. End slaughter. Down 2 for minus 300. It may be one too many.

The hands are then exposed:

North (declarer)
♠ A K
♥ J 9 6 3 2
♦ 8 7
♣ J 9 7 5

West
♠ Q 10 6 3
♥ A Q 7
♦ J 10 9 3
♣ K Q

East
♠ J 8 7
♥ K 10 8
♦ A K 2
♣ 10 8 6 3

South (dummy)
♠ 9 5 4 2
♥ 5 4
♦ Q 6 5 4
♣ A 4 2

C. Results:

We got a zero on a top of four.

North-South Pair Number	Contract	Made	Down	North-South Points	North-South Matchpoints
1.	3NTE		1	+100	3½
2.	3NTW		1	+100	3½
3.	1NTE	2		-120	2
4.	1SW	3		-140	1
5. (us)	2HN*		2	-300	0

3NT does not make (or so it seems). You tell me how a pair stopped in one spade. I can't figure it out.

II. What Should Have Been:

A. The bidding:

This is really a tough one. I think that North's overcall is not without merit, though I realize there would be disagreement about that. I think that if you exchange the jack of clubs for the queen of hearts it would be a better bid. But, as the cards lie, I think it is defensible, but just barely. It is certainly borderline and no better. What tipped me over was the playing strength compared to the defensive strength, and the vulnerability. Lots of potential losers, though.

It turns out that West's 1NT opener put North-South in a bad way. East has an immediate count on the hand and knows that he has a 1 in 3 chance of having 26 points. At most tables, due to the lack of the 1NT opening, the East-West players would be guessing as to whether or not they have the requisite points for game (two pairs went and two didn't). To that degree we got fixed by the specificity of the 1NT opening.

Then, when North intervened, East probably assumed the chances of game were reduced (West was less likely to have 15 highs and North sits behind declarer) and decided to settle for the double and the plus. We gave them one option they did not have.

My guess is that, had I not intervened, we would have had no better than an average minus anyhow. But, you never know. East may have carried on to game or might have bid 2NT and West may have carried on. East decided to play for the sure score.

B. The play:

It appears that North can do no better than down 2 for minus 300. The play of the hand is therefore incidental.

Lessons:

1. Consider "weak notrump" bids as balanced low openers and not as weak hands to be ignored.

2. As we note from the East-West bidding, in marginal games one should be conservative. This is the same theme we have seen before (on hands 3 and 9).

3. The more specific the bid (in terms of point count and distribution), the easier it will be for partner to gauge the total strength of the hand and place the contract.

17. Double Dribble

Week 17
Board 17
None vulnerable
North Dealer

Again, this is the last round of the evening on a 5½ table Mitchell night. We've had a week of ice storms, so people are feeling the release from their houses for the first time and a break from cabin fever. We've had a respectable evening so far (except for one very bad round). Jo and I are both in playing moods.

I. What Happened:

A. The bidding:

I pick up my usual in first position:

North (me)
♠ 8 7 2
♥ Q 2
♦ Q 6 5 3 2
♣ K 7 3

Seven highs with no spots. Pass. East bids one club, partner doubles and West passes. I bid 1 diamond (shows 0-8 points and no 4-card major). East doubles and partner bids 1NT which is passed out.

The Bidding

N	E	S	W
pass	1C	double	pass
1D	double	1NT	pass
pass	pass		

B. The play:

West leads the jack of hearts. Now, shown is the hand as Jo Ann saw it:

North (dummy)
♠ 8 7 2
♥ Q 2
♦ Q 6 5 3 2
♣ K 7 3

South (declarer)
♠ A Q 9 5
♥ 8 7 5 3
♦ A K
♣ 10 6 4

Jo went up with the queen and the defense cashed a quick four heart tricks, followed by the lead of the eight of clubs through North's king. East plays the jack which holds (after Jo plays the three from dummy). A spade switch is taken by Jo's queen. She cashes her top two diamonds and then a small spade from her hand to LHO's ten. Another club is pushed through and then they cash three clubs for down three. They got four clubs, four hearts and a spade.

C. Results:

We got the bottom I anticipated. In this volume, we must keep in mind, it is not what "the experts" do, it is "what should have happened" that is really important. . . . what one could do in a similar circumstance (lessons to be learned). Therefore, let's take it easy on Jo this time.

The hands are exposed:

North (me)
♠ 8 7 2
♥ Q 2
♦ Q 6 5 3 2
♣ K 7 3

West
♠ 10 3
♥ J 10 9 6
♦ J 8 7 4
♣ 9 8 2

East
♠ K J 6 4
♥ A K 4
♦ 10 9
♣ A Q J 5

South (partner)
♠ A Q 9 5
♥ 8 7 5 3
♦ A K
♣ 10 6 4

112

North-South Pair Number	Contract	Made	Down	North-South Points	North-South Matchpoints
1.	1NTE	1		-90	1
2.	1CE	1		-70	2
3.	1NTN	1		+90	4
4.	3HW		1	+50	3
5. (us)	1NTS		3	-150	0

II. What Should Have Been:

A. The bidding:

I think that the bidding in the case of North, East and West is fairly standard. It is the bidding of South which is very questionable. First of all, her double of one club is correct. She has support for both majors and both high honors in diamonds. After the double of one diamond, she should pass and wait for the call by West. She appears to be much better placed for defense than offense. If she has any call to make (which I would not do), it would be two diamonds for preemptive pruposes. If LHO bids one heart, which might get passed around to her, she could bid two diamonds. If RHO raises LHO's one heart to two or one spade to two, she might pass. If LHO bids two clubs, she might venture two diamonds. But, to bid 1NT is 1) to indicate stops in three suits (particularly when RHO has indicated strength in them; and, 2) to show much more than she has point-wise. It is a distinct overbid and a misbid. How is that for being gentle? She did not give East-West the chance to misbid.

B. The play:

In my opinion, the hand was misplayed as well. First of all, Jo got the lead of the jack of hearts. She should have asked herself, why the jack of hearts rather than a club? What does West have in hearts to lead the jack? She knows that there are seven hearts in the East-West hands. East probably has at least three for her double of one diamond. Therefore, it is probable that West has four. (With four spades and three hearts a spade would be led.) Therefore, she is marked with better hearts than clubs, better hearts than spades, and probable diamonds (three or more). If Jo places West with four hearts (as seems likely from the lead), she must then think of what they might be. Probably she lacks the ace or king (from the lead of the jack). If so, East has ace-king third. Therefore, not covering the jack will mean that when West continues with the ten (presuming East lets the jack ride) to the queen and king, the suit will be blocked. East is then shut out of the West hand and must lead from his strength. This is a lot to think about on opening lead, admittedly; is easier double-dummy (for sure). But, what has Jo got to gain by covering? Play an honor only for a reason. If she then covers the second round of hearts, East can cash her third heart. Then what? Jo can win the spade switch with the queen, play her ace-king of diamonds, and go into the tank. When the hearts were not continued, she knew West had four. She (in terms of the bidding as well as probability) has four diamonds (she also sees East drop the ten and nine of diamonds), so she has five cards in the black suits. Perhaps four spades and one club, but not four clubs or clubs would have been led (but a spade was not led), or perhaps three of one and two of the other (most likely). If West has three spades (to the ten, for example), the winning play is ace of spades and out a spade. East will be forced to win and be endplayed in clubs. Or, if West has two spades, the play will work. She has nothing to lose by playing that way. What she does not want to do is establish com-

114

munication for East and West. She did that at trick one by covering the jack with the queen. If, however, West has three spades to the jack, East and West will get the other heart, but Jo could stand one lead through her clubs and still endplay East. As the cards lie, she should hold the defense to three hearts, two spades and a club. She gets three diamonds, two spades and one club. Notice that that adds up to twelve tricks. Whether she makes it or goes down one depends upon sluffing. She will have +90 or -50. An average or a top. If West sluffs the diamond when East cashes the last spade, the contract will be made; otherwise, it will go down one. There is really nothing magical about the play. The key is just finding out what is meant by the lead and what the opponents are likely to hold. Easier said than done.

Lessons:

1. The opening lead (along with the bidding) may provide the key to effective declarer play. Why did the defender on lead choose that card?

2. Bidding your points twice (double dribble) gains nothing and sacrifices partnership trust.

3. Bidding notrump after the opposition has indicated strength in a particular suit or suits (when you don't hold stops in those suits) will lose in the long run.

4. Picking a partner with a sense of humor is essential in writing a book like this one.

18. A Long Dummy Suit

Week 18
Board 18
North-South vulnerable
East Dealer

We have a six and one half table Mitchell movement tonight and this is our first round. Two women with ability but little sophistication to their game are sitting East-West and greeting us with the usual "howdy". For all of us a good first round seems to be very important . . . it rather builds confidence and sets the tone.

I. What Happened:

Another dog.

```
              North (me)
          ♠  J 8 3
          ♥  J 9 3
          ♦  6 4 3
          ♣  Q J 6 3
```

LHO is the dealer and opens with one diamond. Partner passes and RHO bids one spade. After my pass, LHO bids three diamonds. RHO bids three spades, and LHO raises spades to four.

The Bidding

N	E	S	W
—	1D	pass	1S
pass	3D	pass	3S
pass	4S	all pass	

B. The play:

I'm on lead and have very little to go by and no clear cut lead. What I don't want to do is to lead one of their suits. If we have some tricks, we had better take them off of the top because dummy may have a runable diamond suit.

A heart or a club? I pick a club in hopes of catching the king in dummy. When dummy is exposed I note that a heart may have been better.

North (me)
♠ J 8 3
♥ J 9 3
♦ 6 4 3
♣ Q J 6 3

East (dummy)
♠ K Q 4
♥ A 7 2
♦ K Q 9 7 5 2
♣ 8

Partner grabs her ace and switches to a trump. Declarer wins in dummy and leads a low diamond from the board. Partner grabs her ace felling the jack and switches to a heart. Declarer takes her king, ruffs a club and plays the queen of spades from dummy (partner showing out). She then plays the king of diamonds and pitches a club. A ruff of the five of diamonds enables declarer to draw my last trump. A heart to the ace of dummy, and the diamonds are good and declarer has nothing left but trumps . . . making five. Looks average to me.

C. Results:

Average. A fairly flat board, for a change.

North-South Pair Number	Contract	Made	Down	North-South Points	North-South Matchpoints
1.	4SW	5		-450	2½
2.	4SW	4		-420	5
3.	4SW	7		-510	0
4.	5SW	5		-450	2½
5. (us)	4SW	5		-450	2½
6.	4SW	5		-450	2½

The hands are exposed:

North (me)
♠ J 8 3
♥ J 9 3
♦ 6 4 3
♣ Q J 6 3

West (declarer)
♠ A 10 9 7 6 5
♥ K 8
♦ J
♣ K 9 4 2

East (dummy)
♠ K Q 4
♥ A 7 2
♦ K Q 9 7 5 2
♣ 8

South (Jo Ann)
♠ 2
♥ Q 10 6 5 4
♦ A 10 8
♣ A 10 7 5

As to why pair two only made four is a bit of a mystery. It could have happened a variety of ways. North-South pair number three managed to hold it to seven. Apparently the aces were not taken. Perhaps a trump lead followed by a diamond which held. Then declarer may have ruffed out the ace or led the king of diamonds which may have been covered and ruffed. In any event, five is normal.

II. What Should Have Been:

A. The bidding:

There is not much to comment upon here. In a way the bidding is standard, although some may have preferred that East raise spades immediately rather than jump re-bid diamonds — a matter of choice, I think.

B. The play:

North's lead is disputable although not unstandard. The main question pertains to South's return of a trump after the taking of the ace of clubs. South, looking at the dummy, most fears the setup of the diamond suit and the ruffing of clubs in dummy. She must know that (given her singleton trump and dummy's three and declarer's announced length of five or more) North has four or fewer trumps. Probably North has three or four spades. If he has three, a trump lead may hand declarer control of the hand. She could win in dummy, knock out the ace of diamonds and still have entries. A diamond lead does not help. The only thing left is a heart. If North has the king, it may be possible to knock out the ace before the ace of diamonds is unlocked, and then a heart trick or two cashed. Then, it would be held to four or even set one trick. Returning a trump destroys the timing and gives control to declarer with plenty of time to accomplish her objectives. South should play North for the king of hearts . . . her only hope. Note that nothing is lost if he lacks that.

Note also that declarer took a dangerous line of play. After knocking out the ace of diamonds drawing two rounds of trumps, she cashed the king of diamonds before ruffing one in her hand. She was still missing the jack of spades at that point. She could have been overruffed coming back to her hand. She should have ruffed a diamond immediately. She had no reason to do other than that.

Lessons:

1. When defending a hand, one should try to foresee what the declarer is likely to do with the hand and try to thwart that. In this case, that means cutting the communication with the dummy (knocking out the ace of hearts).

2. When defending a hand, it is often necessary to establish a suit for your side before the declarer knocks out your stopper in his suit (so you can cash your winners before he discards them on dummy's suit). In this case, pushing hearts may help (it does not in this case as the cards lie).

3. When dummy has a long establishable suit, it is important to knock out communication with the dummy.

4. When dummy has a long establishable suit, it is necessary not to miss the cashing of aces when necessary. (With respect to N-S pair 3, the failure to take the ace of diamonds was silly).

5. It is possible to find fault with your partner's play and bidding on any evening if you look hard enough. The beauty of writing a book is that you have total control and the last word.

19. Splitting Your Honors

Week 19
Board 19
East-West vulnerable
South Dealer

We have an eleven pair Howell movement this week, so we face a pair of ladies who normally sit North-South. They have been playing together for 30 years, so inexperience and partnership misunderstandings are not a problem. They are among the best at the club. Talk about standard, standard American. They play it well. No gadgets.

I. What Happened:

A. The bidding:

I look at eleven highs on this one.

North (me)
♠ K 3
♥ 9 5 2
♦ K Q 7 6 2
♣ K 7 4

Partner passes as does RHO. Lacking spade control, I pass. LHO opens with one diamond. Hey, that's my suit! There goes partner making the right lead. West bids 2NT and East, not fearing our defense, carries on to 3NT.

The Bidding

N	E	S	W
		pass	pass
pass	1D	pass	2NT
pass	3NT	all pass	

B. The play:

It's my lead after all. What a choice. I surely don't want to lead her suit (and mine). RHO has announced stops in the other three and I hold the kings. If I lead a heart (and a major seems to be called for) partner would be finessable anyhow. I pick the heart suit. Now for the card. Rather than mislead partner, I pick the top of nothing (the nine). Dummy is spread.

North (me)
♠ K 3
♥ 9 5 2
♦ K Q 7 6 2
♣ K 7 4

East (dummy)
♠ A Q 10 7
♥ K 10 4
♦ A 9 4
♣ J 10 2

Not a real diamond suit after all. My knees got weak when I saw dummy. I kind of expected that the average North would have led a diamond, even if it happened to be bid by LHO. Why she opened one diamond rather than one club is a bit mysterious. Anyhow, my nine goes to declarer's jack. She then leads the three of diamonds from hand and I smoothly insert the queen, which is taken by the ace of dummy (partner dropping the ten and North his teeth). What would have happened if I had not played the queen is interesting — probably a loosing finesse of the nine. But, queens don't mean much in this game, anyhow. This looks like a hand I may regret. Perhaps if I bargain with Jo she'll let me keep this one off the books in exchange for one of hers. No luck. I already see the glee in her eyes. The four of diamonds is led from dummy to the eight of declarer and I grab my king (before it goes away), partner pitching a club. I then slyly exit with a diamond. Declarer leads the jack of clubs to partner's queen and her ace. A finesse of the queen of spades is followed by a good ten of hearts and a king of hearts to the ace and a good queen of hearts from declarer's hand. Anyhow, it's all over (making five). That's right. Five. All we got was the king of clubs and the king of diamonds. Both my tricks. Where were you, partner?

C. Results:

Despite our bidding restraint, we got a bottom.

North-South Pair Number	Contract	Made	Down	North-South Points	North-South Matchpoints
1.	3NTE	3		-600	3
2. (us)	3NTW	5		-660	0
3.	4HW	4		-620	2
4.	3HW	4		-170	4
5.	3NTW	4		-630	1

The hands are exposed:

North (me)
- ♠ K 3
- ♥ 9 5 2
- ♦ K Q 7 6 2
- ♣ K 7 4

West (declarer)
- ♠ 5 4
- ♥ A Q J 3
- ♦ J 8 5 3
- ♣ A 8 3

East (dummy)
- ♠ A Q 10 7
- ♥ K 10 4
- ♦ A 9 4
- ♣ J 10 2

South (Jo Ann)
- ♠ J 9 8 6 2
- ♥ 8 7 6
- ♦ 10
- ♣ Q 9 6 5

Notice that West responded 2NT to 1 diamond instead of bidding 1 heart or 2 hearts. She didn't even have spades stopped. What a bid! Notice, as well, that when East played the hand, 3NT did not do as well. Notice that notrump typically does better than hearts. It is happenstance, of course, that South has a better lead to make than North, but where the notrump was played had an effect upon the score received. And, whether to play in notrump or hearts was a major decision in terms of the matchpointing. If we had held it to four instead of five, we would have still not done well. Therefore, the bidding is most important, although the play did have some effect.

II. What Should Have Been:

A. The bidding:

I have no comments not already made.

B. The play:

Is it really necessary to go into this? Oh well. The opening lead is not abnormal. It is specifically the play of the queen of diamonds on the first lead of diamonds. Inexcusable.

Also, if West had responded one heart, East had then bid one spade and West had then bid 2NT, North would probably have made the more productive lead of the club four. But, that is another matter.

Lessons:

1. Think ahead about what you should do if certain plays materialize. That way you won't hesitate and give your hand away and won't make silly mistakes.

2. It is a good idea, for partnership harmony, to make a real blunder once in a while.

20. You Won't Get Rich

Week 20
Board 20
Both vulnerable
West Dealer

Tonight we have a seven table club championship and we face two women on this, our first round. As North I pick up these cards:

North (me)
♠ K 10 6 5 4
♥ K J 10 7
♦ J 9
♣ J 10

I. What Happened:

A. The bidding:

My RHO passed. I did also. My LHO opened with one club, which partner passed. RHO bids one diamond. I have 9 highs and 5-4 in the majors. I stick in a somewhat risky double. LHO bids two clubs (which takes partner off the hook). I have made my point to partner without

damage. Partner passes and RHO bids three clubs. Shock!
LHO bids five clubs. (Either she underbid with her two
clubs or overbid with five clubs. She either has more than
the 13-15 she first indicated, or has it and decided that
15 and 12 is enough for 5 clubs.) At this point, I think
we must get a good board out of this.

The Bidding

N	E	S	W
			pass
pass	1C	pass	1D
double	2C	pass	3C
pass	5C	all pass	

B. The play:

Partner leads the three of hearts and dummy comes
down:

North (me)
♠ K 10 6 5 4
♥ K J 10 7
♦ J 9
♣ J 10

West (dummy)
♠ J 3
♥ 9 8 5 2
♦ A K 3 2
♣ A Q 2

West had 14 highs and passed in first position, then

followed a one club opener with one diamond. They may have missed a slam.

In any event, declarer played low from dummy and captured my king with her ace. (I assume partner has the queen from the lead of the three.) Declarer then leads the queen of diamonds, and follows with a club to the ace, all following. Then she plays the queen of clubs from dummy, all following. Then she plays her two top diamonds and discards two small hearts. She then leads a heart from dummy to her queen! (They missed a 4-4 heart fit.) She runs her clubs, cashes the ace of spades and yields one at the end to my king of spades, making six. (At this point let me put Jo Ann's mind to rest. . . she won't be criticized for her play or bidding on this hand.)

The hands are exposed:

North (me)
- ♠ K 10 6 5 4
- ♥ K J 10 7
- ♦ J 9
- ♣ J 10

West (dummy)
- ♠ J 3
- ♥ 9 8 5 2
- ♦ A K 3 2
- ♣ A Q 2

East (declarer)
- ♠ A 2
- ♥ A Q 6 4
- ♦ Q
- ♣ K 8 7 6 4 3

South (Jo Ann)
- ♠ Q 9 8 7
- ♥ 3
- ♦ 10 8 7 6 5 4
- ♣ 9 5

East had 15 highs (about what was expected, though she failed to mention the hearts). The results are in, and we did, as expected, better than average.

C. Results:

North-South Pair Number	Contract	Made	Down	North-South Points	North-South Matchpoints
1.	3CW	6		-170	5
2.	6SN*		5	-1400	0
3.	5CW		1	+100	6
4.	4HE	5		-650	1½
5. (us)	5CE	6		-620	3½
6.	4HE	4		-620	3½
7.	4HE	5		-650	1½

Notice that playing the major was at least as good, and often much better, than playing the minor despite the defender's distribution and the lack of length. (East-West had eight hearts and nine clubs and North had four hearts.) In a major suit you only need to make "4" to get the same number of points that comes from making "6" in a minor. You won't get rich playing in minors. Notice also that one pair sacrificed at six spades. I know who they are, but I'm not telling. Notice also that one pair was held to down one in five clubs. Not only did they find a five club contract, but they went down! Apparently, they didn't play the queen of diamonds before cashing the ace-queen of clubs. Then they took the heart hook, cashed the queen of diamonds, and couldn't get back to dummy for the ace-king of diamonds. Some magic.

II. What Should Have Been:

A. The bidding:

West may bid one diamond to open. East should bid one heart. West should raise to two, and East then bid four hearts, period. West has no reason not to open and East has no reason to hide the heart suit.

131

B. The play:

East erred in the play, despite the fact that she made six. She had a shot at seven. She should, after taking her ace of hearts, cash the diamond queen, cash top clubs in dummy and then the top diamonds, pitching a heart and a spade. Then, she should ruff a diamond to get back to her hand. After the run of all of her clubs, she is left with queen-small in hearts and the ace of spades. North has no idea of how many hearts South began with, but he might assume (should) that South has the queen. Should he protect the heart or the spade? Should he keep king-small in spades and one heart or jack-small in hearts and bare his king of spades? He will probably protect his king. Therefore, the small heart is good and declarer makes seven, beating the heart bidders who make four. Big deal.

Lessons:

1. To score well at duplicate it is necessary to play in major suits rather than minor suits, where possible. The name of the game is find that major suit fit even if it is slightly inferior (in terms of length) to the minor suit fit.

2. If a declarer has a known loser and the rest winners, it is a good idea for the declarer to run off his winners in such a way that the defenders are unable to get a count on the hand. (By pitching two hearts on the diamonds, East's hand was countable.) Even though the declarer may not think a squeeze is possible, it may appear to the defenders as though they are being squeezed. And, nothing is lost by proceeding in this way.

21. A Lady with No Escort

Week 21
Board 21
North-South vulnerable
North Dealer

Tonight we meet a couple of gentlemen we have met before.

A. The bidding:

In first position I pick up a classic hand:

North (me)
♠ A Q J 8 4 3
♥ 8 4
♦ 10 8 7
♣ K 9

I hold ten highs, a six card spade suit headed by ace, queen, jack, no void or outside four card suit, and vulnerable in first position. Partner should know fairly closely what I have by a weak two bid. A classic hand.

After my weak two bid, all pass. I bought it.

N	E	S	W
2S	pass	pass	pass

B. The play:

LHO opens the queen of clubs, as a nice dummy appears.

North (declarer - me)

♠ A Q J 8 4 3
♥ 8 4
♦ 10 8 7
♣ K 9

South

♠ 10 7 2
♥ A 9 3 2
♦ 6 2
♣ A 10 8 3

The reader may want to take stock at this point. How would you play the hand?

I assumed that the lead was from queen-jack and that a further lead through LHO (a finesse of the jack) would give me the opportunity to dispose of the losing heart. With that in mind, I won in hand with the king and led the "9" from my hand. I overtook the "9" with the 10 of dummy, intending to play the ace next to get rid of the heart. Surprise! RHO took his jack. He then cashed the two top diamonds and switched to the seven of clubs. What do you play now? I assumed I could always dispose of the heart later, so I played my jack of spades. LHO discarded the nine of diamonds. Do you now assume that RHO has the king of spades? I did. I led the ten of diamonds and ruffed in dummy. I then led the ten of spades from dummy and surprise number 2, RHO is void in spades! That means that LHO had K-X-X-X. He let the ten ride. I then cashed the ace of hearts and the ace of clubs, pitching a heart, as LHO trumped with his six. LHO then led the queen of hearts which I ruffed. They had already won a spade ruff, 2 diamonds and a club, and LHO still had the K-J of spades, making 2 for a plus 110.

What do you think we got for our efforts?

C. Results:

A "1"

North-South Pair Number	Contract	Made	Down	North-South Points	North-South Matchpoints
1.	5DE*		3	+500	5
2.	3DW	3		-110	0
3.	3SN	3		+140	2½
4.	3SN	3		+140	2½
5. (us)	2SN	2		+110	1
6.	4HW		3	+150	4

Two other pairs played in spades, making three. Even if we make three, we do no better than average. The key to whether or not North-South get good boards is whether or not East-West bid too high.

Looking at all four hands:

135

North (declarer)
♠ A Q J 8 4 3
♥ 8 4
♦ 10 8 7
♣ K 9

West
♠
♥ J 10 7 5
♦ A K J 4
♣ J 7 5 4 2

East
♠ K 9 6 5
♥ K Q 6
♦ Q 9 5 3
♣ Q 6

South (dummy)
♠ 10 7 2
♥ A 9 3 2
♦ 6 2
♣ A 10 8 3

After a two spade bid and two passes, West couldn't seem to find a bid (with "10" highs and a void in spades). I admit, if I was West, I would have doubled.

II. What Should Have Been:

A. The bidding:

I see nothing wrong with the bidding by North-South. It seems standard to me. We may have been fixed by the lack of bidding by East-West. Or, if North fails to open, West may bid after three passes and East-West may find their way to the clouds. In any event, we may have received a left-handed gift.

B. The play:

You figure this one out. Did I err in dummy play? Just looking at the hands, without the lead, it seems that declarer must lose one heart, two diamonds and one spade. With the lead of the queen of clubs, declarer thinks he can hold that to making four. Instead, he makes two. How would you have interpreted the lead of the queen of clubs? What would you have done? I believed the (not double-dummy) declarer bid and played the hand properly, except North should have let the 9C ride instead of overtaking with the ten. (Sometimes it is tough to say you did a decent job.) Perhaps my vision is limited, but I'd probably go the same way again.

This is not to say that East did not defend well. He did. However, the lead of the queen from queen-X is not usually recommended. Nor is it productive in the long run to pass with the West hand. We were done in.

Lessons:

1. Although experts will rarely lead queen from Q-X without reason, it appears to be the case that the non-expert will do that. In fact, the non-expert may often be counted on to lead his short suit, of whatever quality, in order to try for ruffs (unless headed by a king), I have found.

2. It is often productive, in terms of defense, not to over-ruff when the opportunity presents itself. Usually you will get another chance anyhow and may promote a lesser trump (as happened here). If East had overruffed the jack, North would have made "3" like the rest of the world.

22. Overcalling

Week 22
Board 22
East-West vulnerable
East Dealer

We meet a new pair this week. They have recently joined the ACBL, and seem to be doing quite well despite a lack of experience.

I. What Happened:

A. The bidding:

My LHO passed in first position, as did partner in second and RHO in third. I have 15 highs but lack real balance:

North (me)
♠ 10 6 2
♥ A J 3
♦ A 7
♣ K Q J 4 3

My five card suit is a minor. So, with tongue in cheek, I open one notrump. (Notice: We have changed our system. We no longer play a variable notrump. We now open a standard 15-17 point notrump in both vulnerable and non-vulnerable positions.) After a pass by LHO, partner bids two diamonds (transfer) and, following a pass, I bid two hearts, which is passed out.

The Bidding

N	E	S	W
	pass	pass	pass
1NT	pass	2D	pass
2H	all pass		

B. The play:

LHO leads the jack of diamonds, as Jo lays her perfect transfer down:

North (declarer - me)

♠ 10 6 2
♥ A J 3
♦ A 7
♣ K Q J 4 3

South (dummy - Jo)

♠ 7 4
♥ Q 9 8 7 4 2
♦ Q 2
♣ 10 9 6

I play low from dummy and take the trick with the ace, RHO following low. I then play a club to the ten which holds. A heart back for the finesse loses to LHO's king. She then cashes the ace of clubs, and exits with the three of diamonds. RHO wins and plays the case club for LHO to ruff. Back comes the ten of diamonds and I am back in control. I pitch a spade from dummy and ruff in my hand. I then play the ace of hearts and run clubs, pitching the last spade from dummy, making 3 for a +140.

C. The results:

With a top of five, we got a three (slightly above average).

North-South Pair Number	Contract	Made	Down	North-South Points	North-South Matchpoints
1.	2HS	2		+110	2
2.	4SW		2	+200	4½
3.	3HS		1	-50	½
4.	3SW		2	+200	4½
5. (us)	2HN	3		+140	3
6.	3CN		1	-50	½

The hands are exposed:

North (declarer)
♠ 10 6 2
♥ A J 3
♦ A 7
♣ K Q J 4 3

West
♠ A Q J 9 3
♥ 10 6
♦ K 8 4
♣ 7 5 2

East
♠ K 8 5
♥ K 5
♦ J 10 9 6 5 3
♣ A 8

South (dummy)
♠ 7 4
♥ Q 9 8 7 4 2
♦ Q 2
♣ 10 9 6

Both East and West had decent suits and never opened their mouths. I would like to take this opportunity to thank them.

II. What Should Have Been:

A. The bidding:

It is debatable whether or not North should open one club or one notrump. I chose 1NT because it has preemptive value and because it is descriptive in terms of point count. Further, with transfer bids available, we have tools to deal with responses to notrump openers . . . and those tools are very specific (such as Lebensohl). When the opposition is vulnerable, and you are not, you may buy the contract at a low level . . . as they may be afraid to intervene.

South's transfer is perfect. The question is, should East or West have intervened? Given the sequence, I believe it is debatable (with value on both sides) that East and/or West could have intervened. To do that vulnerable you need good values and a good suit, and both have that. Furthermore, it is unlikely that you will get doubled in a non-expert game. Also, interference may force the opposition to go a bit overboard. I believe that West (in the pass out seat) might have ventured two spades after the response to the 2D transfer. Then, North-South are at a guess. West presumes that the points are fairly evenly divided or North-South would have ended up in game. Why let them pick the trump suit? Note that if North-South go to the three level, East-West get a good board, with proper defense. Letting them (in terms of part scores) name the trump suit and bid with no interruption is generally losing strategy.

B. The play:

The lead of the jack of diamonds is normal. North should, however, play the queen (in case East led from K-J-10). A low club to the ten is a nice play, as the ace is unlikely to be played and an entry is needed for the heart hook. If the ace is played, and a club continued, North should win in dummy with the nine and finesse the heart. As the hand materialized, after the ruff of the club, East should have a count on North's hand (in terms of point count). North has shown up with the jack of hearts (and the presumed ace), the ace of diamonds, and the K-Q-J of clubs (for 15). He probably has at most the queen of spades. If he had had the ace-queen of spades instead of the ace of hearts, he would not have bothered to go to dummy with the ten of clubs for a heart hook. Therefore, the proper switch is the king of spades. In that way, East-West get two spades, a diamond, a heart, a club, and a club ruff. The contract should go down one (giving East-West a tie for top).

Lessons:

1. Getting a point count on declarer's hand (when he opens a notrump) will, during the hand, help the defense to place certain cards with partner. This will help the defenders make switches of suits when necessary.

2. Opening one notrump has an advantage of letting partner know your strength and balance and preempting the opponents, especially when they are vulnerable. Furthermore, there are many specific bidding tools which can be used following a notrump opener (either with or without interference) which will help you arrive at the best

contract.

3. In terms of competing for part scores, letting the opposition name the trump suit with no bid of interference is generally losing strategy.

23. Four Openers

Week 23
Board 23
Both vulnerable
South Dealer

I. What Happened:

A. The bidding:

As North I pick up a nice playing hand:

                    North (me)
                    ♠ K Q 10 7 6 4 3
                    ♥ Q 5
                    ♦ A J 10
                    ♣ A

Partner and RHO both pass. I elect to open four spades, which is doubled by LHO as all pass.

The Bidding

N	E	S	W
		pass	pass
4S	double	all pass	

B. The play:

To my delight, East opens the queen of diamonds, which I win in hand.

North (me)
♠ K Q 10 7 6 4 3
♥ Q 5
♦ A J 10
♣ A

South (dummy)
♠ 8
♥ K J 7 4
♦ K 8 5 4 2
♣ 10 6 5

I then lead the queen of spades which wins, West dropping the jack, which appears to be a real card. I count two spades and one heart loser unless East gets a ruff, which may erode his natural spade trick. I therefore lead the king of spades next, which loses to the ace, RHO pitching the nine of clubs. Back comes a small club to my ace. I then play the ten of spades and out a spade, RHO pitching a diamond on the last spade. Back comes a club, which I ruff. I play jack of diamonds and a ten to the king and get two heart pitches on the long diamonds. . . making five. That should be a top.

C. Results:

As expected, we did get a top.

Howell movement

North-South Pair Number	Contract	Made	Down	North-South Points	North-South Matchpoints
2.	4SN	4		+620	1½
4.	4SN	4		+620	1½
5. (us)	4SN*	5		+990	4
7.	4SN	4		+620	1½
10	4SN	4		+620	1½

Whether or not we make five makes no difference. Just making the doubled contract got us the top. The hands are exposed:

North (declarer)
♠ K Q 10 7 6 4 3
♥ Q 5
♦ A J 10
♣ A

West	East
♠ J	♠ A 9 5 2
♥ 10 9 3 2	♥ A 8 6
♦ 9 7 6	♦ Q 3
♣ Q J 9 8 7	♣ K 4 3 2

South (dummy)
♠ 8
♥ K J 7 4
♦ K 8 5 4 2
♣ 10 6 5

Despite the 4-1-1 spade split, 4 spades is cold.

II. What Should Have Been:

A. The bidding:

North has a choice, one spade or four spades, as I see it. The advantage of one spade is that one may not get overboard. The advantage of four spades is that partner may have fewer than six points and four spades will make (he may have passed out one spade) and it has interference and preemptive value. I selected the four level opener, although there may be some legitimate disagreement as to which is the best approach. I know we are short of slam, or at best it is marginal (and therefore, as we have seen, not the matchpoint play to bid it) so that four spades is our limit. Bidding four directly leaves East, if he has anything, at a guess in terms of bidding and leading. Let them make the guesses.

Further, in terms of the double, East has none. Periodically, the best bid over a preempt is "pass". Take your medicine. Don't try to rescue or try for a top. He has a passed partner and has no idea of the content of North's hand. He has no double.

B. The play:

East is looking for a couple of tricks. Leading the queen from queen-X is rarely a good lead (somewhat amateurish). The best defense in his position may have been a passive one. In effect, he exposed a missing honor without provocation. As one can see by the hand, it greatly simplifies matters for declarer.

Lessons:

1. After partner has passed, four level openers, when not too dangerous, have the advantage of preemption and interference.

2. Doubling preempts may be risky. It is sometimes bet-

ter policy to just take your medicine and to quietly pass along.

3. It is normally a bad lead to lead queen from queen-X.

24. Doubling A Notrump

Week 24
Board 24
None vulnerable
West Dealer

I. What Happened:

A. The bidding:

Another Howell movement tonight (five tables). I like a Howell because you get to play against just about everyone. In any event, my RHO opens with a 13-15 point notrump. I look at my hand and find 14 highs:

                    North (me)
                 ♠ 7 6 4 2
                 ♥ A K 5
                 ♦ A J 7 4
                 ♣ Q 6

I double, LHO passes and partner bids two hearts, which ends the auction.

The Bidding

N	E	S	W
			1NT (13-15)
double	pass	2H	all pass

B. The play:

RHO leads the king of spades as I spread my hand.

North (dummy - me)
♠ 7 6 4 2
♥ A K 5
♦ A J 7 4
♣ Q 6

South (declarer - Jo Ann)
♠ A 10 5
♥ J 9 8 7
♦ Q 9 3
♣ J 8 3

Jo wins the king of spades in hand with the ace. She next leads the three of diamonds to dummy's jack, which holds the trick. This is followed by the ace of diamonds and a diamond to the queen and king. Back comes the queen of spades, followed by the nine to Jo's RHO's jack. Her RHO then plays the ace of clubs followed by a club to the notrump opener's king. He then leads a small heart which Jo ducks to her jack. She then leads a heart to the king followed by the ace, and gets the news that hearts are 4-2. She then leads the case diamond and pitches from her hand, LHO ruffing . . . and she is down one.

C. Results:

In the five table Howell movement, we got a one.

North-South Pair Number	Contract	Made	Down	North-South Points	North-South Matchpoints
2.	2SN	2		+110	4
4.	2HS		1	-50	1
5. (us)	2HS		1	-50	1
7.	2NTS		1	-50	1
10.	1HS	1		+80	3

The hands are laid down:

North (dummy - me)
♠ 7 6 4 2
♥ A K 5
♦ A J 7 4
♣ Q 6

West
♠ K Q 9
♥ Q 10 6 3
♦ K 6 5
♣ K 10 2

East
♠ J 8 3
♥ 4 2
♦ 10 8 2
♣ A 9 7 5 4

South (declarer)
♠ A 10 5
♥ J 9 8 7
♦ Q 9 3
♣ J 8 3

North-South had the contract each time. They went down three of the five times they got the bid.

II. What Should Have Been:

A. The bidding:

Jo Ann and I have an agreement that a double of a notrump opener (in direct) position indicates a notrump opener. However, this was a 13-15 point opener. We might say that the double of a 13-15 point notrump opener indicates an equivalent hand. On average, Jo would assume that between West and North there are 28 high cards, or so. She has eight. She therefore must assume that North-South have the balance of points . . . 22 or so. Further, she must assume that East has very little, so that the majority of the East-West points are concentrated in the West hand. If she would happen to pass the double, she must assume that West would have to play the hand largely out of his own hand. I believe that she should pass the 1NT doubled. It turns out, however, that East has a five card suit, and West has a fit for that suit . . . and they may therefore make 1NT . . . unless they get a diamond lead. With a diamond lead we take a spade, two hearts, three diamonds and a club, for down one. Otherwise, it appears they have a chance to make. A diamond lead, though, is called for, as less help is need by North from South, and North thinks West may have to play the spades out of his hand. When your side has the balance of points, it is often a good idea to pass out their doubled notrump opener.

B. The play:

From the looks of the hand, declarer must lose two spades, one heart, one diamond and two clubs, for down one. It is possible, however, given the spade lead, to establish a long spade for a pitch of a losing diamond on the long spade, providing East does not ruff. Then, West would be ruffing with a good heart . . . for a loser on loser play. The play of a couple of rounds of trumps before the play in spades (the fourth round) would ensure that. In general terms, however, barring such a play, two hearts will go down one.

Lessons:

1. When a notrump opener is doubled (showing an equivalent hand), it is often a good idea to pass out the double if your side has the balance of points.

2. When leading against notrump, leading a suit in which you need little help from partner for its establishment is a good idea (rather than a suit needing lots of help from partner).

3. When you are declarer, it is a good idea to count your winners and to try to figure out where the necessary tricks might possibly come from.

25. A Preempting Partner

Week 25
Board 25
East-West vulnerable
North Dealer

We are nearing the end of our North-South experience, and we face two women we have seen before. I pick up what seems to be my average.

North
♠ Q J 7 6 4
♥ K 10 7 3
♦ 5
♣ J 5 3

I. What Happened:

A. The bidding:

After my pass, East makes a vulnerable three diamond bid (in second seat). Partner passes and RHO bids five diamonds. No further bids.

N	E	S	W
pass	3D	pass	5D
all pass			

B. The play:

Partner is on lead and she picks the seven of diamonds. Dummy is exposed and it seems from my hand that, if partner has the king of clubs, we may have a chance to beat this.

North (me)
- ♠ Q J 7 6 4
- ♥ K 10 7 3
- ♦ 5
- ♣ J 5 3

West (dummy)
- ♠ A 10 8 5
- ♥ 8 5
- ♦ K 8 4
- ♣ A Q 8 6

Declarer wins the diamond in hand and then cashes the ace, all following except me. Then declarer leads the ten of clubs to the queen, which holds. She then cashes the ace of clubs, followed by a heart to her queen and partner's ace. (I played the ten on the heart lead.) Partner leads a heart back to my king, which holds. If declarer had the jack of hearts, she would claim, as she would only have one spade, unless she has one more club (in which case she may have let the ten ride). But, she doesn't claim, so I assume she has two spades, one of which is not the king. Therefore, I lead a small spade to partner's king and dummy's ace. Declarer then ruffs a club and I say "unless you have a good heart, I'm not going to pitch my spade" . . . down one. She throws it in.

C. Results:

We got a top on this one.

North-South Pair Number	Contract	Made	Down	North-South Points	North-South Matchpoints
1.	5SN*		3	-500	2
2.	3DE	3		-110	3
3.	5DE	5		-600	½
4.	4HS		2	-100	4
5. (us)	5DE		1	+100	5
6.	5DE	5		-600	½

We were the only North-South pair to set five diamonds. Apparently East was given a sluff and a ruff with a heart return.

II. What Should Have Been:

A. The bidding:

159

Let's take a look at all four hands to see where East-West went wrong.

North
♠ Q J 7 6 4
♥ K 10 7 3
♦ 5
♣ J 5 3

West (dummy)
♠ A 10 8 5
♥ 8 5
♦ K 8 4
♣ A Q 8 6

East (declarer)
♠ 3 2
♥ Q 2
♦ A Q J 10 9 3 2
♣ 10 9

South (Jo)
♠ K 9
♥ A J 9 6 4
♦ 7 6
♣ K 7 4 2

What is proper for a preempt in second seat vulnerable? I would say certainly a good suit. I would also say no more than six losers outside. In my opinion, East has a good preempt. Opposite a second seat vulnerable preempt, what would it take to raise the preempt to five? If the suit is solid (it is presumed that it is or nearly is),

160

the losers outside must be limited to two. Therefore, the raiser must have at least three quick tricks outside and probably closer to four. What does West have? I count 2½ — perhaps one trick short (which turned out to be the case). What about other bids by West? West could pass or bid 3NT. West counts seven diamonds, a club and a spade. If she gets no heart lead she makes 3NT. If she gets a heart lead, and East has 3 hearts and hearts are 4-4, she still makes. If hearts are 5-4, it is possible the defense will block hearts. In any event, she is better off doing that than bidding five diamonds, in my opinion. In the actual case, she may get a heart lead and will go down one with proper defense. However, what about a pass? Plus 110 is a better than average board for East-West. Perhaps passing a preempt with only two of the outside suits stopped and less than three quick tricks on the side is the best action.

B. The play:

East misplayed the hand. First of all, by not unblocking the king of diamonds, she had to ruff a club to come back to her hand after North had made the switch to the spade. This gave North a count on the hand. If she had had a good heart, she could claim. If she had a losing heart, she could ruff it. If she had to ruff the club to return to hand, North knows he has the setting trick in spades. If she had unblocked the king of diamonds earlier, and then had run her diamonds, what would North have saved, the jack of clubs or the queen of spades? He may have guessed wrong and the ten of spades would have been good.

Lessons:

1. When your partner preempts vulnerable (in a minor), you need 3-4 quick tricks outside of the trump suit to raise to game in the minor. To bid notrump, you need two quick tricks (outside of the trump suit) and entries to the dummy's long suit and the other three suits stopped. Lacking the above, a pass is best.

2. When you are declarer, and need one more trick than you can see, think in terms of a possible squeeze . . . and play to set it up. When playing the squeeze, the less you let the opposition know about your hand, the better. The more they know, the easier it will be for them to discard.

26. Balanced Strength

Week 26
Board 26
Both vulnerable
East Dealer

This is the last week of our sitting North-South. Next week we begin to play against the players who normally sit North-South.

I. What Happened:

A. The bidding:

I take a peek at the following, my usual it seems. Matter of fact, most of the people here seem to complain about their hands. No one at our club ever gets good hands, I guess.

North (me)
♠ 10 6 2
♥ 8 7 5
♦ A 5
♣ Q 10 8 4 3

East passes and partner bids one notrump. All pass. I feel as though clubs may be better, but if I bid two clubs that is Stayman. With some other partners we have a system which says that 2NT over 1NT is not invitational, rather a transfer to three clubs. Then responder passes, if that is his suit, and bids three diamonds if he wants to play in diamonds. In exchange, 2NT loses its invitational meaning. Jo and I haven't worked that out yet.

The Bidding

N	E	S	W
	pass	1NT	all pass

B. The play:

Jo's LHO opens the queen of hearts. For the sake of readability I'll describe the hand as she saw it.

North (dummy - me)
♠ 10 6 2
♥ 8 7 5
♦ A 5
♣ Q 10 8 4 3

South (declarer - Jo Ann)
♠ A K 9 3
♥ A K 6
♦ J 10 2
♣ 9 6 5

Jo takes the queen of hearts with the ace. She then plays

the five of clubs to LHO's ace. LHO comes back with a small heart to RHO's ten. She lets that hold. RHO makes a shift to the king of diamonds. Jo wins in dummy and plays the queen of clubs. Her RHO wins with the king as LHO shows out. Back comes the queen of diamonds followed by the nine to her jack, all following except dummy. Jo then plays a small spade toward dummy and LHO produces the jack and RHO overtakes with the queen. RHO then cashes the jack of clubs and two diamonds. Down 2 for -200. This can't be wonderful.

The hands are exposed:

North (dummy - me)
- ♠ 10 6 2
- ♥ 8 7 5
- ♦ A 5
- ♣ Q 10 8 4 3

West
- ♠ J 8 7 5
- ♥ Q J 9 3 2
- ♦ 6 4 3
- ♣ A

East
- ♠ Q 4
- ♥ 10 4
- ♦ K Q 9 8 7
- ♣ K J 7 2

South (declarer - Jo)
- ♠ A K 9 3
- ♥ A K 6
- ♦ J 10 2
- ♣ 9 6 5

C. Results:

North-South Pair Number	Contract	Made	Down	North-South Points	North-South Matchpoints
1.	1NTN	1		+90	5½
2.	1SS	1		+80	4
3.	2CS		1	-100	2
4.	1DS	1		+70	3
5. (us)	1NTS		2	-200	½
6.	3SS		2	-200	½
7.	1NTN	1		+90	5½

We got a ½ on a top of 6 (a near bottom). The question is why?

II. What Should Have Been:

A. The bidding:

The fact that 1NT appears to make when played by North and not when played by South is unfortunate. However, the question is whether or not South should open 1NT rather than 1 in a minor (in this case clubs). South has no stops in the minors. Her strength is concentrated in two suits which are not of sufficient length to bid. With points so concentrated (and such weakness elsewhere), it is often bad policy to open with a bid which implies balanced strength. Not only do you mislead partner, but you invite disaster. If she had opened one club, and if North had a major, she could have raised to two (her three card support for hearts is adequate) or three, depending upon the suit. If she had received a bid of two clubs, she would find herself in the best place, perhaps. Opening 1NT seems to gain nothing for her, and it is nondescriptive. The beauty of the 1NT opener is that it describes a certain type of hand (15-17 points with balanced strength) which enables partner to gauge the hand and decide where it ought to be played.

B. The play:

It is very hard to see how Jo could have made it given the defense. After the diamond switch, she can count six tricks (two spades, two hearts, two diamonds). Getting the extra trick is hard to find. Double dummy, of course, if she cashes her top hearts and spades, can endplay East and pick up another club trick. But, in practice, that may not be the way to proceed.

However, I believe that when she wins the diamond in dummy, she should come to her hand with the spade and lead up to the queen of clubs, instead of just laying it down, hoping to trap the jack (not a winning play). Then, West shows out. East will come back a diamond. Now she leads her ace of spades, not to endplay East, necessarily, but rather to hold it to down one. The endplay works if East has five diamonds and two hearts (which turns out to be the case). Cashing out for down one isn't great, but why not in her position? What has she got to lose?

Incidentally, pair 3 North-South misplayed the two club contract, which should make. South gets two spades, two hearts, two diamonds and two clubs if played correctly. That should be a tie for top.

Lessons:

1. Bid notrump with balanced strength. It is not enough to have 15-17 points.

2. When playing notrump, and the lead comes up to your

ace-king, play the king first. If you had the ace, you would probably hold off the first round. You may not do that with the king alone. It is deceptive.

II. THE HANDS SITTING EAST-WEST

27. A Switch In Time

Week 27
Board 1
None vulnerable
North Dealer

This week we begin our East-West playing. On the one hand, I am looking forward to having stronger bidding competition, and on the other, I don't like to sit out. On balance, this is quite a sacrifice I'm making (and Jo Ann) to ensure randomness so that generalizations made by this study will be more valid.

I. What Happened:

A. The bidding:

Sitting East, I pick up a nice hand:

> East (me)
> ♠ A Q 5
> ♥ K 6
> ♦ A Q
> ♣ J 10 8 7 6 4

Sixteen highs and two doubletons. With two doubletons I elect a one diamond opener. I'm not very consistent in this. Sometimes I would open such a hand 1NT. But, this time it is being recorded, so I had better watch myself. Partner responds one heart. I jump to 2NT and partner carries on to 3. Our opponents pass the entire time.

The Bidding

N	E	S	W
pass	1D	pass	1H
pass	2NT	pass	3NT
	all pass		

B. The play:

LHO leads the four of clubs. Until I see dummy, I feel we may have a problem.

West (Jo)	East (declarer - me)
♠ K J 10 9	♠ A Q 5
♥ Q J 9 4	♥ K 6
♦ 9	♦ J 10 8 7 6 4
♣ K J 5 3	♣ A Q

170

Looking at both hands, I note that we have four spades, four clubs, and two hearts (once the ace of hearts is removed). Making four should be a better than average board. If they find diamonds after they take the ace of hearts, we may not get too good a board. To distract the opponents, I take the club lead in hand with the ace (it may make them think that they own the queen). I then lead the king of hearts, which holds, noting with interest the play of the eight by RHO. I then lead the six to the jack, which wins, RHO kindly playing the ten. I lead the queen off dummy to LHO's ace, and she falls into the trap and plays another club. Now I can rattle off my tricks, making five . . . I got three heart tricks.

C. Results:

Obviously, the diamonds are split between North and South. What surprises me is that three other pairs made five.

North-South Pair Number	Contract	Made	Down	East-West Points	East-West Matchpoints
1. (us)	3NTE	5		460	4½
2.	3NTE	5		460	4½
3.	3NTW	3		400	2
4.	3NTW	5		460	4½
5.	3NTW	5		460	4½
6.	2DE	2		90	1
7.	4SW		2	-100	0

The entire deal is shown:

North

♠ 8 7 4 3 2
♥ 10 8
♦ A Q 5
♣ 9 8 2

West (dummy)

♠ K J 10 9
♥ Q J 9 4
♦ 9
♣ K J 5 3

East (declarer)

♠ A Q 5
♥ K 6
♦ J 10 8 7 6 4
♣ A Q

South

♠ 6
♥ A 7 5 3 2
♦ K 3 2
♣ 10 7 6 4

II. What Should Have Been:

A. The bidding:

Perhaps a 1NT opener would be used by some, but in this case a one diamond opener was chosen. If West had responded with two diamonds or three diamonds, for example, a slam in diamonds would be found, perhaps, and would not as easily be found following a 1NT-3NT auction. Opposite a major suit response, as was expected, a jump to 2NT would still leave the hand with the tenaces (East) as declarer.

B. The play:

It is important for East not to try to set up the diamond suit, which may have been a temptation in one case (at North-South table 3). East should count his winners and realize that it is a losing proposition to give North-South three tricks in diamonds.

In terms of defense, South erred by not switching to a diamond. How should she know that a diamond is called for? What is missing is A-Q of spades, A-Q of diamonds, and queen of clubs. That is 14 highs, of which North has about 5. Now, East bid notrump after a heart response. Therefore, he is marked with a spade stop.

If by chance East has the ace third of spades, a spade switch would hurt North-South. If North has the ace of spades, he will always get that. Therefore, it is pointless to lead spades. If partner has the queen of clubs, declarer cannot set up that suit, either. If any switch is likely to make a difference, it must be diamonds. Even if he leads away from his king, he still will have a diamond stop. And, perhaps the big clue to the necessary diamond switch, East failed to attack diamonds when he had his chance. This places, I would say, North with either the ace or queen (or both) of diamonds. Declarer attacks first, typically, at notrump, those suits they want to set up. The failure to attack a suit is a clue to the defense.

Lessons:

1. If at all possible, gear the bidding in such a way that

the hand with the tenaces becomes the declarer.

2. On defense, attacking the suits avoided by declarer, on balance, is a winning play.

3. "Placing" certain cards in partner's hand often provides the key to winning defense.

28. Leading From A Tenace

Week 28
Board 2
North-South vulnerable
East Dealer

I. What Happened:

A. The bidding:

In this week's six-table game, we are facing a married couple. As the dealer I pick up this hand:

East (me)
♠ 9 3
♥ 10 7
♦ K 9 8 7 6
♣ K J 7 3

I have no bid. My pass is followed by two other passes and a 1NT to my right. LHO bids two clubs. RHO follows with two hearts. LHO bids two spades and RHO retreats to 2NT. LHO pushes on to 3NT, Jo Ann and I being silent the whole time.

The Bidding

N	E	S	W
	pass	pass	pass
1NT	pass	2C	pass
2H	pass	2S	pass
2NT	pass	3NT	all pass

B. The play:

I have to choose a lead . . . a diamond or a club. I pick the fourth best diamond, the seven.

East (me)
♠ 9 3
♥ 10 7
♦ K 9 8 7 6
♣ K J 7 3

South (dummy)
♠ A Q J 8 7
♥ Q 4 3
♦ 5 2
♣ Q 10 9

Partner plays the queen, which wins. She returns the ten which is covered by the jack and won by my king. I then play the nine, which rides to RHO's ace, partner following. Declarer then plays the king of spades, all following, and then the ten of spades. Finally, he leads his third spade to the board and runs the other two spades. On the three spades which require pitches from me, I pitch a heart and two clubs, not in that order. Finally, declarer leads the nine of clubs from the dummy and lets it ride to my jack. I cash two diamonds and he is down one. The hands are then exposed:

North (declarer)
- ♠ K 10 4
- ♥ A 9 6 5
- ♦ A J 4
- ♣ A 5 4

West (Jo Ann)
- ♠ 6 5 2
- ♥ K J 8 2
- ♦ Q 10 2
- ♣ 8 6 2

East (me)
- ♠ 9 3
- ♥ 10 7
- ♦ K 9 8 7 6
- ♣ K J 7 3

South (dummy)
- ♠ A Q J 8 7
- ♥ Q 4 3
- ♦ 5 2
- ♣ Q 10 9

C. Results:

North-South Pair Number	Contract	Made	Down	East-West Points	East-West Matchpoints
1.	4SN	4		-620	1
2.	3NTN	3		-600	2
3.	3NTN	5		-660	0
4. (us)	3NTN		1	+100	4
5.	3NTN		1	+100	4
6.	4SS		1	+100	4

We got a tie for top on a very ordinary appearing defense.

II. What Should Have Been:

A. The bidding:

Certainly Jo Ann and I would have bid the hand differently. We would have first transferred into spades and then the transferer would have bid 3NT, indicating the points for game and a five card spade suit. Then it would have been up to the opening notrump bidder to choose between 3NT and 4 spades. The way the opposition bid the hand, if they ended up in four spades, the big hand would have been exposed and would have lost the advantage of a lead up to the strength.

Should North prefer 3NT or 4 spades with his hand? There seem to be indications for either (and contraindications). In favor of four spades is that the points in the North hand are "primary" (aces and a king in South's suit). With "primary" points, a suit contract tends to be best. Also, North knows they have a 5-3 fit. In favor of 3NT is the one trick less that is needed to make the game, and the idea that, barring a dummy reversal, the "short" hand will have no ruffing power. It will probably play as well in notrump.

Jo Ann and I would have bid the hand as indicated. If I were South with a non-balanced hand and five spades, I would transfer and then bid a suit. Because South did not do that, if I were North I would think South is also balanced and would opt for the notrump contract . . . as North did. However, there seems to be no point for the use of Stayman here.

B. The play:

The lead of East is a bit of a problem. Should he lead his stronger suit (clubs) or his longer (diamonds)? Apparently, some led clubs (those playing at tables 2 and 3). That hands declarer his ninth trick. The standard logic is that one should not (other things being equal . . . whatever that means) lead against notrump from a tenace in a four-card holding, a tenace being K-J or A-Q. It is acceptable from a five-card holding. With five, when partner gains the lead, you may have the four tricks necessary to set the contract.

It is possible, however, that the contract can be made with a diamond lead. If declarer takes the first trick (instead of holding up), and then leads a club, the entry to the East hand is exhausted and North has the protected jack of diamonds. If East rises with the king, declarer has nine tricks. If he does not, declarer still has nine tricks. He may even do that after cashing his spades. He could return to hand with the club ace.

Playing the diamonds and the club as North did, he gave himself no chance for the contract (if diamonds were 5-3). The correct play is to rise with the ace and then (before or after cashing spades) attack clubs. If East has the king of hearts instead of clubs, North is in trouble.

179

North has to guess the suit. I would pick clubs to lead up to because of the intermediates (the nine and ten). It may also have been of value to watch the discarding on the spades. On his first discard East pitched the seven of clubs. North should have then placed East with the king of clubs and acted accordingly. But, by then it was too late anyhow. If North had risen with the ace, it would have been a good idea for East to false card (he might have first pitched the ten of hearts instead of the club to let North think his entry was in hearts).

Lessons:

1. Against notrump, do not (under most circumstances) lead fourth best from a four-card tenace holding.

2. It is not always a good idea to hold up until the third round when acting as declarer in a notrump contract and when holding the ace-jack-third (for example). Rising with the ace and then developing an "avoidance play" will, in effect, give you a second stopper in the suit. (The avoidance play is described above . . . keeping East in the lead so West can't lead through your jack-small holding).

3. If you can see no other way to make the contract, "place" certain cards in your opponents' hands and then play the hand as though that is where they are.

29. Take The Sure Game

Week 29
Board 3
East-West vulnerable
South Dealer

We again face the two women who have been playing as partners for 30 odd years. If we just break even with them, typically, we will be ahead of the field. Despite their lack of gadgets, they seem to score well each week.

I. What Happened:

A. The bidding:

South (my LHO) passes. To my surprise, my partner opens with one diamond.

East (me)
♠ K 10
♥ K 4
♦ Q 7 4
♣ A Q 9 8 7 6

With six clubs to the ace queen (and two doubleton kings in the majors) I bid two clubs. Partner bids two spades. Now I have a choice of 2NT, 3NT, 4 clubs, 4 diamonds or 3 diamonds. I assume her two spade bid shows extra values and denies a stop in hearts. The question is whether we have a slam in clubs or diamonds. Remembering all I learned from the previous hands (note week 9), I decide to go for the sure above average board and play in notrump. Six diamonds may make, but it will rarely be bid at our club. In a tournament, to really score well, it may be necessary to try to make the slam. But here, I bid 3NT and let it go at that.

The Bidding

N	E	S	W
—	—	pass	1D
pass	2C	pass	2S
pass	3NT	all pass	

B. The play:

LHO leads the obvious heart. The ace is played from RHO and dummy comes down:

West (dummy - Jo)	East (declarer - me)
♠ A Q 6 2	♠ K 10
♥ J 9 5	♥ K 4
♦ A K 10 8 5 2	♦ Q 7 4
♣	♣ A Q 9 8 7 6

I note that partner had a nice diamond suit and that the ace of hearts is to the right of my king, so six diamonds will make. I also note that we will beat all who play in five diamonds. In any event, RHO decides to continue the hearts rather than switch to clubs, so my king wins the trick. Things break well, so I rattle off one heart, one club, six diamonds, and four spades LHO had pitched a spade on the run of the diamonds, making six.

C. Results:

As I figured, we end up with an above average board.

North-South Pair Number	Contract	Made	Down	East-West Points	East-West Matchpoints
1. (us)	3NTE	6		+ 690	4
2.	3NTE	6		+ 690	4
3.	3NTE	6		+ 690	4
4.	3NTE	6		+ 690	4
5.	5DW	6		+ 620	½
6.	3NTE	6		+ 690	4
7.	5DW	6		+ 620	½

North
♠ 9 8 7
♥ A 10 6 2
♦ 9 3
♣ J 10 4 2

West (dummy)
♠ A Q 6 2
♥ J 9 5
♦ A K 10 8 5 2
♣

East (declarer)
♠ K 10
♥ K 4
♦ Q 7 4
♣ A Q 9 8 7 6

South
♠ J 5 4 3
♥ Q 8 7 3
♦ J 6
♣ K 5 3

The slam depended upon the ace of hearts being in the North hand (a 50% shot). Why gamble with a 50% shot for 6 when you can get a sure 4? Percentage-wise, it is a losing proposition. Play for the above average game.

II. What Should Have Been:

A. The bidding:

The local game makes it right in terms of percentages to go for the notrump game and take the above average board. It may have been necessary in a regional contest to explore for the slam. However, even there the percentages favor a notrump contract. One is less dependent upon the lie of the ace of hearts. I feel as though East, in all his wisdom, did the right thing.

B. The play:

There is very little to the play (as far as East-West are concerned). When six diamonds are run by declarer, South has a problem . . . what to protect? She has to save the queen of hearts (as the jack is in dummy), the king protected in clubs, and therefore has little choice but to pitch a spade or bare her king of clubs. She was in a bad way.

Lessons:

1. When faced with a choice of an uncertain slam or a fairly sure notrump game (in a local contest), play for the game.

2. The partner who has the most information about the two hands and the point count should place the contract, where possible, to avoid the chance that his partner may misinterpret the bids and/or get overboard. In this case, East needed to protect the king of hearts and knew that slam was no more than a fifty percent chance (given the possibility that the ace of hearts could have been offside).

30. Maximize Your Chances

Week 30
Board 4
Both vulnerable
West Dealer

This week we are blessed with an even nine table game . . . we don't sit out. Nine is a bit big for us . . . but this is the club championship.

I. What Happened:

  A. The bidding:

As the partner of the dealer I pick up the following:

East (me)
♠ K 10 6
♥ K 6 5 2
♦ A 9 8 5 3
♣ 3

Partner opens one club. I respond one heart . . . bidding my major first. Partner jumps to three, and I carry on to four, our opponents silent the entire time.

The Bidding

N	E	S	W
			1C
pass	1H	pass	3H
pass	4H	all pass	

B. The play:

LHO opens the three of spades and partner puts down just what I expected.

West (dummy - Jo)
♠ A 9 5
♥ A 10 7 4
♦ 7 4
♣ A Q J 4

East (declarer - me)
♠ K 10 6
♥ K 6 5 2
♦ A 9 8 5 3
♣ 3

When I first saw dummy, several things crossed my mind. I felt that the contract was probably normal . . . therefore the play and defense would matter. I also felt that, if the Q-J of spades were not in the same hand (except in the South hand), I had just picked up a trick in spades. There did seem to be several ways to approach this hand. What I did was first play low from dummy (which would, via a later finesse, pick up a trick in spades

187

. . . if the honors were divided). I covered the jack with the king. Then, I played a low diamond from hand. LHO won the ten and returned a spade, putting me on the spot right away. Should I finesse? I rose with the ace and led a diamond to my ace. I then ruffed a diamond, all following. Now, the two diamonds in my hand were good, so I played ace of hearts and back to my king. Then a lead of the good diamond enabled me to pitch the spade from dummy. I then ruffed my ten of spades. Then, ace of clubs followed by the queen of clubs, which was not covered, so I ruffed it. I led the last diamond, and the opponents grabbed the queen of hearts, leaving my six good, making five.

C. Results:

A 6½ on a top of 8. Why such a good board? Let's see what happened.

North-South Pair Number	Contract	Made	Down	East-West Points	East-West Matchpoints
1.	3NTW	5		+660	8
2.	2HW	4		+170	4
3.	4HE		1	-100	1½
4.	4HE	4		+620	5
5.	3NTW		1	-100	1½
6.	2HW	2		+110	3
7.	4HE	5		+650	6½
8. (us)	4HE	5		+650	6½
9.	3NTW		2	-200	0

North
♠ Q 8 7 2
♥ J 8
♦ Q 6 2
♣ 9 7 6 2

West (dummy - Jo)
♠ A 9 5
♥ A 10 7 4
♦ 7 4
♣ A Q J 4

East (declarer - me)
♠ K 10 6
♥ K 6 5 2
♦ A 9 8 5 3
♣ 3

South
♠ J 4 3
♥ Q 9 3
♦ K J 10
♣ K 10 8 5

The question is why that happened. Two of the results are a little strange to me. How did one pair make five notrump? You tell me. How did one pair go down two in three notrump? Anyhow, let's see what should have taken place.

II. What Should Have Been:

A. The bidding:

I think it is debatable whether or not West should open up 1NT or 1 club. I prefer the notrump opener because of its specificity and because we have all kinds of gadgets which we can use after an opener of one notrump. Then, after a two club bid by East, and a two heart response by West, East would push on to four hearts.

Why 3 pairs played notrump when East-West have a 4-4 major suit fit and East has a singleton, is a bit indicative of our club's expertise in bidding. I think that the hand should have been played in four hearts from the West side. None did that. How two pairs stopped in two hearts defies explanation. In any event, four pairs did reach four hearts . . . all from the East side. Two made five, one made four and one made two. Why such variance?

B. The play:

I believe that I made a mistake in the play of the hand. The play to the first trick was correct. The ducking of the diamond at trick two also was correct. Then when the spade is played at trick three (noting the lead of the "three" at trick one), East must think he has at least a 75% chance of a finesse. I opted to reject the finesse and follow with the ace of diamonds and a diamond ruff. The chances of diamonds splitting 3-3 are certainly less than 75%. East could have been overruffed and then might have lost a spade. Either East should accept the second round spade finesse or reject it and play diamonds differently. He should first (at trick four) cash two top hearts and then play ace of diamonds and ruff one. Or he might even take the spade hook and then play diamonds differently. The way he played diamonds, he just got lucky. But, it did not matter that much. Even making 4 would have given E-W 5 matchpoints. At least cashing a couple of top hearts (hoping for the 68% chance of a 3-2

190

split) before the diamond play would have removed some of the threat of an overruff and then the cashing of the spade.

Lessons:

1. Opening 1NT with relative balance gives partner a very specific idea of your hand, therefore making arrival at the right contract more certain.

2. Reaching a 4-4 major suit game is best, especially when one or both hands has some ruffing power.

3. If you think there is a chance of being overuffed (while trying to set up a side suit), to maximize your chances of success, first cash a couple of trumps to eliminate the chance that a person short in the suit being ruffed (and behind the ruffer) is also short in trump. He then can't overruff.

31. With A Singleton

Week 31
Board 5
North-South vulnerable
North Dealer

My partner is gone this week. It happens to be her anniversary and she still doesn't have her priorities right, I guess. In any event, I have a new partner to introduce to you. His name is Bucky Brooks and we have played in several tournaments together. Basically, we play the same system as do Jo Ann and I. (Bucky is a math and computer professor at Delta State . . . my university.)

In any event, we have 8½ tables tonight.

I. What Happened:

A. The bidding:

Against a married couple I pick up these cards:

East (me)

♠ J 10 8
♥ 10 9 6
♦ Q 10 7 5 3 2
♣ A

Another hand with little potential. Habits must be hard to break. In any event, I am surprised by my RHO's call of 3C. She's trying to keep me out of slam, I guess. Well, I pass. My LHO carries on to 3NT. That is passed around to me. I kind of feel I have a decision to make, though perhaps I don't. Because of my stiff ace, lack of other controls and the favorable vulnerability, I feel as though I should bid four diamonds, which I do with senseless abandon. Believe it or not, that buys it (undoubled).

The Bidding

N	E	S	W
3C	pass	3NT	pass
pass	4D	all pass	

B. The play:

LHO leads the king of hearts as dummy comes down with a shocker:

West (Bucky - dummy)	East (declarer - me)
♠ A 6 5	♠ J 10 8
♥ J 8 2	♥ 10 9 6
♦ A J 8 6 4	♦ Q 10 7 5 3 2
♣ 7 3	♣ A

It first occurs to me that I would have received a diamond lead against 3NT. Then, when in with my ace of clubs we would have taken five diamonds and a spade for down three, had I just passed 3NT. LHO probably has king and one diamond and RHO preempted with a void. Well, dummy plays low to the heart and RHO drops the queen! Could it be that RHO has five spades and a void and preempted in clubs? I'm confused. On the ace of hearts RHO pitches a small club. LHO continues with a small heart. Dummy plays the jack and RHO produces the king of diamonds. LHO must have bid 3NT with a singleton diamond. A club return is won by the ace. I draw the outstanding trump and lead the jack of spades which is covered and won by the ace. A spade back is led to my eight and LHO's nine and I also lose the ten of spades for down 2 (-100). Strange!

A hard way to get an average. Take a look at these hands:

North
- ♠ 7 4 3 2
- ♥ Q
- ♦ K
- ♣ K Q J 9 8 5 4

West (dummy)
- ♠ A 6 5
- ♥ J 8 2
- ♦ A J 8 6 4
- ♣ 7 3

East (declarer)
- ♠ J 10 8
- ♥ 10 9 6
- ♦ Q 10 7 5 3 2
- ♣ A

South
- ♠ K Q 9
- ♥ A K 7 5 4 3
- ♦ 9
- ♣ 10 6 2

North-South Pair Number	Contract	Made	Down	East-West Points	East-West Matchpoints
1.	5CN		1	+ 100	4½
2.	6CN*		2	+ 500	6
3.	3HS	4		-170	1
4.	3CN	5		-150	2
5.	5CN		1	+ 100	4½
6.	5CN*	5		-750	0
7. (us)	4DE		2	-100	3

195

North preempted with a four card spade suit and eleven highs. It has been my experience that inexperienced players will preempt whenever they have a seven-card suit, no matter what else they have. It is instinct. South, for his contribution, with six hearts A-K, three clubs to an honor and a singleton diamond (to say nothing of K-Q-X of spades) could find no better bid than 3NT. How should I have guessed that?

II. What Should Have Been:

A. The bidding:

In my opinion, East's bid is a close one. South should, I believe, in response to 3C, bid 3 hearts. North could bid three spades and South could bid four hearts or four spades. In any event, the whole hand is a joke. North should not preempt with a side four card suit in first position, especially a major. If South had had four spades and a nice hand, they may have missed a major suit game. Playing disciplined preempts in first or second seat prevents your partner from having to guess.

B. The play:

Nothing extraordinary here.

Lessons:

1. Never preempt in first or second seat with a side four card suit, especially a major.

2. After partner has preempted, indicating a non-balanced hand, converting to notrump with a singleton in one of the other suits is asking for trouble.

3. When playing against inexperienced opponents, be prepared for surprises.

32. The Right Bid?

Week 32
Board 6
East-West vulnerable
East Dealer

This week Jo is gone, so I called up a former partner of mine, Artie Kamien, to play. Artie has not done a lot of reading, and so we play basically a VERY simple system. In a 7½ table game, we sat out the first round, so we meet pair number one at table one with board six. I pick up another mediocre hand:

```
                         East (me)
                       ♠ 6 5 3
                       ♥ 7 6 2
                       ♦ K J
                       ♣ A 9 5 4 2
```

I. What Happened:

A. The bidding:

As dealer I pass, of course. South does the same. West,

Artie, sticks in a 1NT bid (15-17). The North lady inter-
jects two hearts. Boy, do I have a problem now. We don't
play Lebensohl, I don't have hearts stopped, we appear
to be short of the points for 3NT, I have no strong suit
to bid . . . what should I do? What is the right action?
Because we seem to lack the strength for 3NT, I decide
that double may be the right action . . I just can't let them
buy it at 2H when we have at least 23 points. Can I? The
double is passed out.

The Bidding

N	E	S	W
	pass	pass	1NT
2H	double	all pass	

Now, what to lead. I opt for the unusual lead of the
king of diamonds. Dummy comes down with more than
declarer had the right to expect. Two honors in trumps.

East (me)
♠ 6 5 3
♥ 7 6 2
♦ K J
♣ A 9 5 4 2

South (dummy)
♠ 10 8
♥ Q J
♦ 10 9 6 4 3 2
♣ Q 10 6

B. The play:

Declarer takes my king with her ace, as partner plays the five. She then leads a small heart to the jack and partner's ace. Partner plays the king of spades as all follow (I contribute the three). That means that partner has shown eleven points. Partner then switches to the seven of diamonds for me to ruff. Declarer pitches a small club as I surprise the crowd with the winning jack of diamonds. I fire back a heart to draw dummy's last trump. Declarer then leads a spade from dummy to partner's ace. The queen of diamonds is ruffed by declarer who then draws the last trumps (pitching a critical club from dummy). She then leads the king of clubs (which I allow to win) followed by a small club which I grab with the ace. I then return a club which declarer ruffs. She then plays the queen of spades and gives one up at the end to Artie, for down one. We get a plus 100, which may not be too good if we can make 2NT.

C. Results:

Strangely, a top.

                    North (declarer)
                    ♠ Q 9 7 4
                    ♥ K 10 9 4 3
                    ♦ A
                    ♣ K 8 3

West (Artie)   East (me)
♠ A K J 2   ♠ 6 5 3
♥ A 8 5   ♥ 7 6 2
♦ Q 8 7 5   ♦ K J
♣ J 7   ♣ A 9 5 4 2

                    South (dummy)
                    ♠ 10 8
                    ♥ Q J
                    ♦ 10 9 6 4 3 2
                    ♣ Q 10 6

North-South Pair Number	Contract	Made	Down	East-West Points	East-West Matchpoints
1. (us)	2HN*		1	+ 100	6
2.	2SW		2	-200	½
3.	1SW		1	-100	3½
4.	2NTW		1	-100	3½
5.	1SW		2	-200	½
6.	2HN	3		-140	2
7.	2NTS		1	+ 50	5

201

It appears that E-W have difficulty making anything, so getting a plus on the board was good for a top or near top.

II. What Should Have Been:

A. The bidding:

The question is, of course, what East's proper bid should be. Playing Lebensohl, he has no less of a problem. I don't have much of an answer for this one. Even I am stumped. Some would say a call of 3 clubs could be right or 2NT forcing to 3 clubs and then pass. As you can see, that would be trouble. Passing may be right (here it probably was). This is a very tough choice in any event.

B. The play:

She could have made her contract. When dummy's diamonds were good, if she had been pitching other than clubs from both hands, she would have had the needed entry to dummy to cash the winning ten of diamonds. Declarer misplayed the hand. She found herself having to give up a spade at the end for no reason.

Lessons:

1. Sometimes even sophisticated bidding systems don't cover all situations.

2. When you have the choice of playing defense or offense, and have points but lack a good bid or good suit

33. A Lesson Not Learned

Week 33
Board 7
Both vulnerable
South Dealer

After a week's hiatus, Jo and I are trying to get back into form for our local sectional. At the second table I pick up these cards:

> East (declarer - me)
>
> ♠ K 9 6 2
> ♥ A Q 9 8 6
> ♦ Q
> ♣ K 10 8

I. What Happened:

A. The bidding:

After two passes RHO opens one spade. I overcall two hearts, which is raised to three by my partner and I carry on to four . . . that ends the auction.

fit (as far as you know), it may be right just to play defense and double your opponents. Getting a plus score will often get you a better than average board.

The Bidding

N	E	S	W
		pass	pass
1S	2H	pass	3H
pass	4H	all pass	

LHO opens the seven of spades and Jo spreads her hand.

West (dummy - Jo)
- ♠ J 8 5
- ♥ J 10 5
- ♦ 8 7 6
- ♣ A Q 3 2

East (declarer - me)
- ♠ K 9 6 2
- ♥ A Q 9 8 6
- ♦ Q
- ♣ K 10 8

B. The play:

My first thought is that I'm going to get ruffed on the return after the ace of spades. I already have planned the duck of the spade return (kind of a loser on loser play). But, surprise, RHO plays the ten and I win with the king. A chance . . . knowing for sure that RHO has the king of hearts, I go to dummy with a club and lead back the jack of hearts which LOSES to LHO. He then leads a diamond to RHO's ace. She then cashes two spades . . . for down one.

C. Results:

An average board.

North-South Pair Number	Contract	Made	Down	East-West Points	East-West Matchpoints
1.	3HE		2	-200	½
2. (us)	4HE		1	-100	3½
3.	4DN	4		-130	2
4.	3HE		2	-200	½
5.	3HE		1	-100	3½
6.	3HE	3		+140	5½
7.	2HE	3		+140	5½

We were the only pair to find our way to game. Isn't that nice?

Let's look at the hands:

North
- ♠ A Q 10 4 3
- ♥ 4 3
- ♦ A J 9 5 3
- ♣ 6

West (dummy - Jo)
- ♠ J 8 5
- ♥ J 10 5
- ♦ 8 7 6
- ♣ A Q 3 2

East (declarer - me)
- ♠ K 9 6 2
- ♥ A Q 9 8 6
- ♦ Q
- ♣ K 10 8

South
- ♠ 7
- ♥ K 7 2
- ♦ K 10 4 2
- ♣ J 9 7 5 4

206

II. What Should Have Been:

A. The bidding:

Not a very tough hand to analyze. I should have stopped at three. If I had, we would have done well above average on this one (if the defense went the same way). Several times before we have found that in close situations it is negative in terms of matchpoints to bid the close game or slam (note hands 3, 9, 13 and 16, for example). I should have known better. Just making four would have been a tie for top whether or not we bid the game.

B. The play:

Nothing remarkable here, although North and South missed the chance to set the contract two tricks. After winning the diamond return, North could cash the ace of spades, realize the position, and lead the three of spades for her partner to ruff. Her partner would pick up the suit preference signal and return a club for North to ruff. They missed that, however. Perhaps not an easy play for them to find.

Lessons:

1. Remembering the lessons to be learned from these hands may pay dividends.

2. Just getting a plus score is often sufficient to get a good board on a hand.

34. A Redundant Bid

Week 34
Board 8
None vulnerable
West Dealer

Just as I am preparing to note this hand, one of our opponents mentions that there is another hand I ought to be writing up (one which he says we will later encounter). It turns out that we (given the 8½ table movement tonight) never would meet that hand. In that hand the North player was dealt a 5-8 minor two suiter. In my attempt to explain the benefits of randomness, I try to demonstrate how some of these apparently boring hands add to the validity of what I'm doing. With that in mind, I pick up this super collection:

East (declarer - me)
♠ Q J 8 6 2
♥ 7 5 3
♦ K 7 4
♣ J 10

I. What Happened:

208

A. The bidding:

Partner opens up with 1NT (15-17). RHO comes in with two clubs. Now it is my turn. Because we play Lebensohl, a bid of 2S is weak (a closeout). Although I think that game is a remote possibility, I think a partial is the limit, so I bid 2S. LHO finds the inconvenient call of 3C which is passed around to me. Now what? Double looks wrong. A bid of three spades repeats my story, and a pass lets them buy the contract, and I have little defense. Given the known minimum of a 5-2 fit (and partner's strength) and partner's probable lack of wasted club values, I opt for the three spade call. After all, I could have had much less than I do for my two spade bid. In any event, three spades buys it undoubled.

B. The play:

I'm given the surprising lead of the nine of diamonds. Dummy comes down with the expected.

West (Jo- dummy)
♠ A K 10
♥ Q 10 9 2
♦ A Q 5 3
♣ 8 4

East (declarer - me)
♠ Q 10 8 6 2
♥ 7 5 3
♦ K 7 4
♣ J 10

If the nine of diamonds is a singleton, which appears to be the case, then they rate to make three clubs. Probably I made a good bid. They would probably lose two spades, a heart, and a diamond (at most). Now, to make three spades. I see eight tricks off the top (5 spades and 3 diamonds). Either I can get the long diamond or develop a heart trick. I win the first trick in dummy with the queen and play the ace of spades. Then, on the king of spades, RHO drops the nine of clubs. So, they had one diamond and one spade to lose. It may make four clubs. I draw two more rounds of spades and play two rounds of diamonds. LHO pitches a club and a heart. RHO had pitched another club and a diamond on the two last spades. The second diamond lead confirmed that LHO had a singleton. After the failure to pick up the diamonds, I lead a diamond from the dummy and ruff it. Then I lead a club. They cash three clubs and two hearts, for down one.

C. Results:

Average.

North
♠ 3
♥ K 8
♦ J 10 8 6 2
♣ A K 9 7 6

West (Jo)
♠ A K 10
♥ Q 10 9 2
♦ A Q 5 3
♣ 8 4

East (me)
♠ Q J 8 6 2
♥ 7 5 3
♦ K 7 4
♣ J 10

South
♠ 9 7 5 4
♥ A J 6 4
♦ 9
♣ Q 5 3 2

North-South Pair Number	Contract	Made	Down	East-West Points	East-West Matchpoints
1.	4SE		3	-150	1½
2.	3HS*		2	+300	7
3.	3HS		3	+150	6
4.	3CN	6		-170	0
5.	2SE	2		+110	5
6.	2SE		1	-50	3½
7.	4SE		3	-150	1½
8. (us)	3SE		1	-50	3½

211

First, I notice that in terms of the bid, three clubs surely makes. I also notice that in terms of the play, none made any more than we did. Of those who played in spades, three pairs were held to making "1" and two pairs made "2". If our play was not bad (by comparison) and our bidding not incorrect (though perhaps unorthodox), why did we get an average?

II. What Should Have Been?

A. The bidding:

I think it is the job of East to bid three spades, not the job of the notrumper to raise East. For all West knows, East could be broke. And, West has already indicated at least a minor fit for spades, made even more likely by North and South showing that their points are in clubs. Further, East has more of a handle on West's hand than the reverse.

Once the three club bid is made, East-West have a tough time. How two pairs North-South found their way to three hearts is hard to understand. Perhaps, following a 1NT opener, North overcalled in diamonds and South corrected to hearts (which later got raised). In any event, consider that a fix. We could not, it seems, have done much better than we did under the circumstances.

B. The play:

After the diamond lead, and four rounds of spades, East might lead a diamond to the ace and back to the king. Then, with eight in the bag, he could play up to the ten of hearts (instead of leading a club). If South ducks and North wins the king, he may cash two clubs and then give East a ruff in diamonds or clubs. Then, East would lead another heart to South's ace. If South had made the mistake of pitching a club instead of a heart, dummy's queen could have been the ninth trick. The way East played the hand, he gave himself no chance to make the contract. Not well played at all, but apparently as well played as the other East declarers.

Lessons:

1. If one more trick than you can see is needed to make the contract, figure out how it can possibly be made (given a certain lie of the cards), and play to make it.

2. Using Lebensohl, he who has the most information about his partner's hand should be the one to make the redundant bid, if anyone should.

3. The average bridge hand is not one with an eight-five distribution.

35. Ruffing Power In Dummy

Week 35
Board 9
East-West vulnerable
North Dealer

I. What Happened:

A. The bidding:

North is the first to pass, and I follow suit with my sparse holding:

```
                              East (me)
                              ♠ Q J 9
                              ♥ J 7 6 3
                              ♦ Q J 10 5
                              ♣ 10 2
```

LHO bids one club. Partner overcalls one spade, I bid two spades, and we buy it at that.

The Bidding

N	E	S	W
pass	pass	1C	1S
pass	2S	all pass	

B. The play:

Jo's LHO leads the two of hearts.

West (declarer - Jo)
- ♠ A K 10 6 4
- ♥ K
- ♦ K 8
- ♣ K 9 8 5 4

East (dummy - me)
- ♠ Q J 9
- ♥ J 7 6 3
- ♦ Q J 10 5
- ♣ 10 2

Jo plays small from dummy and drops her king on RHO's ace. RHO returns a heart which she ruffs. She then plays the king of diamonds, which holds. Jo follows with a spade to the queen and then a club to her king, which wins. She then pushes back a club to ten and ace. RHO fires back a spade to her ten and dummy's nine. She then ruffs a club in dummy. She leads the ten of diamonds from dummy, which holds. When RHO covers the jack of diamonds with the ace, she pitches a club. Then the nine of hearts goes to queen of LHO, Jo pitching another club. She claims with the ace and king of spades in her hand . . . making three.

C. Results:

Below average.

North-South Pair Number	Contract	Made	Down	East-West Points	East-West Matchpoints
1.	3SW	3		+140	2½
2. (us)	2SW	3		+140	2½
3.	1SW	4		+170	4½
4.	1NTW	2		+120	1
5.	2SW	4		+170	4½
6.	4SW		1	-50	0
7.	4SW	4		+620	6

Three pairs made four spades and two pairs made three.

North
- ♠ 8 3 2
- ♥ Q 10 4 2
- ♦ 9 6 4 2
- ♣ 6 3

West (declarer - Jo)
- ♠ A K 10 6 4
- ♥ K
- ♦ K 8
- ♣ K 9 8 5 4

East (me)
- ♠ Q J 9
- ♥ J 7 6 3
- ♦ Q J 10 5
- ♣ 10 2

South
- ♠ 7 6
- ♥ A 9 8 5
- ♦ A 7 3
- ♣ A Q J 7

II. What Should Have Been:

A. The bidding:

Let's evaluate Jo's hand after the one club opener by RHO and East's support of her spades. With the power to her right, she rates to have kings which might be upgraded to aces, as the aces are either in partner's hand or her RHO's. If she does upgrade her kings, she may have as many as 18 highs. But, with one king singleton, full value should not be given there. She may have 16-18 points in high cards plus a point or so in distribution. Partner, hopefully, will have some ruffing power for the clubs. However, she sees that she may lose three aces plus, perhaps a club that she can't ruff (or even an ace on the wrong side). Therefore, despite her apparent strength, game rates to be marginal . . . in my opinion. She may have a high marginal game bid here; but, as we have seen, in marginal situations, playing it safe is winning strategy. We note by the results, by the way, that bidding less than 4 and making 4 is worth a 4½ on a top of 6. In my opinion, Jo made a good bid by passing. It was probably easy to be tempted to press on with her hand.

B. The play:

First, of all, let's defend Jo Ann a little bit here. She was indeed unfortunate not to get a club lead (the suit her RHO had bid). Perhaps everyone else did . . . and that makes it easy to make four. She instead got a heart lead, which makes things considerably more difficult.

But, given the lead she did receive, where Jo made a mistake, I feel, is in entering dummy with a spade at trick three. After the king of diamonds hold, she should play another diamond. She may need the spades in dummy for a ruff. Let's say they grab the second diamond. They now have won a diamond and a heart. Now what? If they push back a spade, you can win in dummy and lead a club. If they grab that and lead another spade, you win on board, a club to king. A club ruff, a diamond, pitching a club, another diamond with another pitch of a club, ruff a heart and claim. You will have made two heart ruffs, three diamonds, the king of clubs, a club ruff, and three spades . . . making four. With all of the high trumps, and the lack of balance in her hand, she should think in terms of the ruffing power of dummy, rather than in terms of the drawing of trumps. She needed one more ruff in dummy . . . and the entering of dummy with the spade precluded that. Notice that if RHO returns another heart instead of a spade, it makes her job even easier. Or, if he fails to take the diamond at trick two, she has an easy go of it. What she does not want to do, herself, is to draw trump.

Lessons:

1. When you hold all of the high trumps and an unbalanced hand with a non-runable side suit, think in terms of ruffing in dummy.

2. It is not necessary to push for game with marginal hands in order to get a good board.

36. The Master Suit

Week 36
Board 10
Both vulnerable
East Dealer

East (me)
♠ K Q J 8 7 6 2
♥ 10 3
♦ K 10 5
♣ A

I. What Happened:

A. The bidding:

In first position I note the writing on the wall. It seems as though most of the East players will open with four spades. Because I have the highest ranking suit, I see no need to rush it, so I open one spade. LHO doubles (making me glad I did not rush it) and RHO bids 1NT (partner passing). I can handle defending 1NT, I think, so I pass. LHO doesn't want to, however, so he bids two clubs, which is passed to me. I bid two spades. That is passed around to RHO who then bids three clubs. I inject three spades, which buys it.

The Bidding

N	E	S	W
	1S	double	pass
1NT	pass	2C	pass
pass	2S	pass	pass
3C	3S	all pass	

B. The play:

The king of hearts is led.

West (dummy - Jo)
- ♠ 10
- ♥ 8 7 6 5 4
- ♦ Q 4 3 2
- ♣ Q 6 3

East (declarer - me)
- ♠ K Q J 8 7 6 2
- ♥ 10 3
- ♦ K 10 5
- ♣ A

LHO cashes two hearts (despite my efforts to stop her

. . . I even played the three on the first trick). She continues with the queen which I ruff. Let's see now: I have lost two tricks, still have the ace of spades to lose and the ace of diamonds. The key is not to lose two diamonds. I plan to lead to the queen of diamonds and finesse the ten coming back (if all goes well). First things first. I lead to the ten of spades, but RHO grabs it. Back comes a club to my ace. I then pay two more rounds of trumps (all following) and then lead the fateful diamond to the queen. LHO grabs her ace, ending any problem. Making three.

C. Results:

I expect a good board here, because they can make three clubs or go down just one. Or, if East-West buy the contract, they won't make more than three, I expect, and may have bid it to four. Actually, we end up with just a little over average (anything over average in a game this size is good). If we did that on all boards (only ½ point over average), we would end up with a score two boards over average. So, I'll take it.

North-South Pair Number	Contract	Made	Down	East-West Points	East-West Matchpoints
1.	3SE	3		+ 140	3½
2.	4CN		1	+ 100	2
3.	3CS	3		-110	0
4. (us)	3SE	3		+ 140	3½
5.	4CS*		1	+ 200	5½
6.	5CS		2	+ 200	5½
7.	4SE		1	-100	1

North

♠ A 9 3

♥ J 2

♦ J 8 7 6

♣ J 8 7 4

West (Jo)

♠ 10

♥ 8 7 6 5 4

♦ Q 4 3 2

♣ Q 6 3

East (me)

♠ K Q J 8 7 6 2

♥ 10 3

♦ K 10 5

♣ A

South

♠ 5 4

♥ A K Q 9

♦ A 9

♣ K 10 9 5 2

What messed us up is that three of the North-South pairs bid on to four and five clubs.

II. What Should Have Been:

A. The bidding:

Because North and South have both bid clubs, and East

has the singleton ace and length in spades, he should not, in my opinion, sell out to three clubs (as did the East at table number 3). If West has anything, it rates to be in diamonds or hearts, and therefore useful. But, East is taking a chance going to four, or opening with a four level bid . . . with no support (note pair 7). When North-South go to the four level, West may double (or even East). But pass may be right at the four level. The name of the game, though, is re-evaluation when you have a playing hand with no wasted values in their suit. Don't sell out cheaply.

B. The play:

The only mistake in the play is when South went up with the ace of diamonds on the first diamond lead by East. She knows the ace won't go away and that East has no place to park it. East is marked with seven spades, two hearts, at least one club (but not three), and therefore at least two diamonds. If East is missing the jack, he may err and play the king on the way back, giving North a trick in diamonds and the setting trick, incidentally.

Lessons:

1. When you have a strong playing hand and no wasted values in the opponents' suit, it pays to not sell out cheaply.

2. When a card is led to the queen in dummy, and you have the ace as LHO, and if declarer is marked for at least two cards in the suit, you have no reason to play the ace on the first round (other things being equal).

3. If you control the master suit (opening hand and seven cards in the suit), it is not usually necessary (other things being equal) to jump right to the four level. You can take your time (case out the lie of the points so you don't get overboard).

37. Don't Go Overboard

Week 37
Board 11
None vulnerable
South Dealer

I. What Happened:

  A. The bidding:

Against a non-systematic pair of men in a seven table evening, my LHO (South) opens with a call of one spade. Partner passes and RHO gives a two over one of two hearts.

East (me)

♠ Q 9
♥ 8 5
♦ A K 10 7 6
♣ 10 6 4 2

Not strong enough for a call of three diamonds, I pass. LHO bids three clubs. RHO repeats his hearts at the three level and all pass . . . short of game.

N	E	S	W
		1S	pass
2H	passs	3C	pass
3H	all pass		

B. The play:

I'm on lead and the ace of diamonds jumps out of my hand.

East (me)

♠ Q 9
♥ 8 5
♦ A K 10 7 6
♣ 10 6 4 2

South (dummy)

♠ A K 7 4 2
♥ 2
♦ 9 4
♣ K Q 9 5 3

Partner plays the three on my ace, so I switch to the queen of spades. Declarer then cashes the king of spades and pitches a diamond. He then leads the two of hearts, successfully finessing the jack. He then plays the ace of hearts, all following except the dummy. When he leads the seven of hearts, partner takes the ten. She returns the queen of diamonds followed by the jack, declarer ruffing the third round. A club to the king and ace puts partner back on lead. She returns a spade which declarer ruffs. Declarer gives up the king of hearts and claims. Down one. He lost two hearts, a club and two diamonds.

C. Results:

Not a very good board:

North-South Pair Number	Contract	Made	Down	East-West Points	East-West Matchpoints
1.	3SS		2	+ 100	3
2. (us)	3HN		1	+ 50	1½
3.	4HN		3	+ 150	5
4.	5CS		3	+ 150	5
5.	3CS	4		-130	0
6.	3CS		1	+ 50	1½
7.	5CS		3	+ 150	5

North (declarer)
♠ 10
♥ A Q J 9 7 3
♦ 8 5 2
♣ J 8 7

West (Jo)
♠ J 8 6 5 3
♥ K 10 6 4
♦ Q J 3
♣ A

East (me)
♠ Q 9
♥ 8 5
♦ A K 10 7 6
♣ 10 6 4 2

South (dummy)
♠ A K 7 4 2
♥ 2
♦ 9 4
♣ K Q 9 5 3

South had the wisdom to stop before they got too high on a possible misfit. In a sense, we got fixed by their "inability" to reach game.

II. What Should Have Been:

A. The bidding:

I think that both South and North did the prudent things. Given the strength of the heart suit, North should rebid them despite the two suited showing of South. He figures to have entries to the South hand and perhaps a doubleton in hearts. South, for his part, stopped after showing his point count and a 5-4 or 5-5 hand. He felt he might have gone overboard on a misfit by continuing to bid. He passed at a good time.

B. The play:

The only mistake in the play belongs in Jo's lap. When one's partner plays the ace from ace-king, and you hold the queen-jack-X or Q-J-X-X or more, you should drop the queen. Then, your partner can underlead the king to put you on lead. Certainly the play of the "3" indicates making a switch. If she had played the queen, I would have led a low diamond to her jack. She then could either play the ace of clubs or return a heart. If she returns a heart, there may be no change in the play of the hand (or its consequences) . . . we still take two hearts, a club and two diamonds. If she continues diamonds, it is possible that a forcing game could be established or at least a heart finesse would not have been possible. In any event, East would then have had one more option than he did have. Probably, however, down one would be the result. If, however, East had had a heart trick, the contract might have been set by two tricks with the play of the ace of clubs after the low diamond to the jack.

Lessons:

1. After you describe your hand in terms of points and in terms of the distribution of your hand, and partner bids again a suit you have shown nothing in, other things being equal, passing may be the right bid. To continue to describe the same thing will often get you overboard.

2. When your partner leads the ace from ace-king, and you hold the queen-jack-X, play the queen to the first trick. He can then underlead his king.

38. No Notrumps?

I. What Happened:

A. The bidding:

Tonight we have a 7½ table Mitchell game, and we face a pair of gentlemen who periodically give us fits. My partner is the dealer and opens 1NT. In effect, most of the time, that marks me as the dummy. No big thing. I will probably be less subject to criticism that way. In any event, I have a nice hand opposite a notrump opener.

East (me)
♠ 9 8 2
♥ Q 10 8 3
♦ A K J 8
♣ Q 10

I make my normal call of 2C. Partner responds with a 2D. I then close out at 3NT . . . our opponents silent the entire time.

The bidding:

230

N	E	S	W
			1NT
pass	2C	pass	2D
pass	3NT	all pass	

B. The play:

Partner gets the lead of the king of spades.

Declarer (Jo)
- ♠ A 7
- ♥ A J 7
- ♦ Q 10 7 5 2
- ♣ A 8 7

Dummy (me)
- ♠ 9 8 2
- ♥ Q 10 8 3
- ♦ A K J 8
- ♣ Q 10

Jo can count eight tricks off the top (a spade, a heart, a club and five diamonds). The question is, where can she get the ninth before they get in with their spades? What she does is this: She wins the second spade and plays off the three top diamonds in dummy (her LHO pitching a low heart on the third). She then leads the queen of hearts from dummy and RHO covers. Jo wins the trick, cashes two more diamonds, the jack of hearts from hand, leads to the ten of dummy and also cashes the eight and finally comes back to her club ace, making five. She lost one spade and one trick at the end (a club).

C. Results:

What would you guess we got on this one? Wrong. We got a six on a top of six. "Why" is a fair question. Let's look at the hands and the results.

North
- ♠ K Q J 6
- ♥ 6 4 2
- ♦ 9 4
- ♣ 9 6 3 2

West (declarer - Jo)
- ♠ A 7
- ♥ A J 7
- ♦ Q 10 7 5 2
- ♣ A 8 7

East (dummy - me)
- ♠ 9 8 2
- ♥ Q 10 8 3
- ♦ A K J 8
- ♣ Q 10

South
- ♠ 10 5 4 3
- ♥ K 9 5
- ♦ 6 3
- ♣ K J 5 4

North-South Pair Number	Contract	Made	Down	East-West Points	East-West Matchpoints
1.	2DE	5		+ 150	1½
2.	5DW		1	-50	0
3.	4HE	4		+ 420	4½
4. (us)	3NTW	5		+ 460	6
5.	5DW	6		+ 420	4½
6.	3DW	5		+ 150	1½
7.	2HE	4		+ 170	3

It is hard to believe that we were the only ones playing in notrump. How the E-W pair at table number one happened to play it from the East side is a bit mysterious. My guess is that it was incorrectly entered on the traveling score sheet. The answer to why we did so well may lie in "what should have been."

II. What Should Have Been:

A. The bidding:

We have extensively discussed the advantages of opening with a one notrump bid when possible (especially with a five card minor and stops in the majors). Here we see the perfect example. (Note that Jo and I have changed our system so that a non-vulnerable notrump opener is now no different from a vulnerable one . . . 15-17 highs. We used to play, you may remember, that non-vulnerable was 12-14.) Apparently what happened is that (if one was a misprint) six of the Wests chose to open with one diamond. Perhaps four of the Easts then supported diamonds and two bid hearts. It is imaginable that West then supported hearts if hearts were mentioned or carried on in diamonds if given a diamond raise. Notrump may never have been considered. In more sophisticated clubs or in tournaments, of course, notrump would be the contract at most of the tables. Not here. Jo certainly made the best bid.

B. The play:

Not much here. Either the king is on side or it is not. The ony slight modification Jo might have made would have been to play the queen of diamonds from her hand first and then run the other three diamonds from dummy. She would then have the advantage of having North-South make one more pitch before the heart hook. If the hook had lost, they might then have pitched a good spade or perhaps given her some other option. Not a big deal though.

Lessons:

1. As we learned in Week 20 (Hand 20), explore the minor suit game only when all other options are unavailable. Taking a chance on notrump is usually better than the minor suit game, unless there is an indication that notrump won't stand a chance.

2. Opening with 1NT, when holding a five card minor and stops in both majors (but not 2-2 in the majors) has many advantages over opening with a minor.

39. Crowd The Bidding

Week 39
Board 13
Both vulnerable
North Dealer

Sitting East in a nine table game, I pick up this hand:

East
♠ K J
♥ A 7 4 3
♦ J 7
♣ Q 10 6 4 2

I. What Happened:

A. The bidding:

My RHO passes and so do I. LHO opens one spade.
Jo overcalls two clubs. North bids two diamonds. I bid
three clubs. LHO goes to three hearts. Jo keeps going
with four clubs. North bids four hearts, where it dies.

The Bidding

N	E	S	W
pass	pass	1S	2C
2D	3C	3H	4C
4H	all pass		

Everyone got into this action.

B. The play:

Partner leads the ace of clubs and dummy is spread.

North (dummy)
♠ 9 7 4
♥ K 9 8 2
♦ K Q 10 9 3 2
♣

East (me)
♠ K J
♥ A 7 4 3
♦ J 7
♣ Q 10 6 4 2

Declarer ruffs the opening lead in dummy and then leads the eight of hearts from dummy. Partner pitches the three of clubs as the queen wins in declarer's hand. Another heart is played, which I duck. I win the third round. I then switch to the king of spades, which is taken by the ace of the declarer.

The jack of hearts draws my last trump. Declarer then plays ace of diamonds, diamond to the king (my jack falls), and he claims . . . making six.

C. Results:

Not good. A 1½ on a top of 8. Hard to believe. Let's look at all four hands and try to figure out why.

North (dummy)
♠ 9 7 4
♥ K 9 8 2
♦ K Q 10 9 3 2
♣

West (Jo)   East (me)
♠ Q 10 2   ♠ K J
♥   ♥ A 7 4 3
♦ 8 6 5   ♦ J 7
♣ A K 9 8 7 5 3   ♣ Q 10 6 4 2

South (declarer)
♠ A 8 6 5 3
♥ Q J 10 6 5
♦ A 4
♣ J

North-South Pair Number	Contract	Made	Down	East-West Points	East-West Matchpoints
1.	3CW		1	-100	7½
2.	3DN	4		-130	6
3.	5DN	5		-600	4
4.	4SS	4		-620	3
5. (us)	4HS	6		-680	1½
6.	6CW*		2	-500	5
7.	5CW		1	-100	7½
8.	5HS	6		-680	1½
9.	5H*S	6		-1050	0

Notice that only three pairs found hearts. Why?

II. What Should Have Been:

A. The bidding:

Let's review the bidding: two passes and then one
spade. West's partner has already passed. She has a void
and a seven card suit. She figures that, with no help from
partner, she rates to go down two doubled and vulnerable.
"The rule of 2 and 3" states that a two trick set (with
equal vulnerability) . . . both vulnerable . . . is a good
sacrifice, as they rate to have a game. Jo should bid three
clubs. She simply left them too much room. Surely she
did not hope to find a game. Why not crowd their bidding? What would North do? Three diamonds, perhaps?
Or three spades? Say either. East then could know his
partner is weak with long wasted clubs on defense. They
have a sure game. He should jump to five clubs. Now
what does South do? Make them guess. West should
crowd the bidding and East should continue with that interference. Because West just overcalled (as she might
have done with five clubs and a big hand), East has no
reason to preempt or sacrifice. He does not know that
West is weak on defense and has seven clubs.

238

B. The play:

Nothing extraodinary.

Lessons:

1. When you know they have a sure game, if not too much risk is involved (Rule of 2 and 3), crowd the bidding as much as possible. Make them make the last guess.

2. If your partner preempts and you have much length in his suit, continue the preempt, in most cases.

3. Generally, overcall at the two level with some defense and skip the bidding with little defense.

40. A Revised Count

Week 40
Board 14
None vulnerable
East Dealer

Playing against some very unorthodox (untrained) male players, I pick up a very ordinary holding:

$$
\begin{array}{ll}
& \text{East (me)} \\
\spadesuit & \text{K 8 6 2} \\
\heartsuit & \text{A 8 7 4} \\
\diamondsuit & \text{9 6} \\
\clubsuit & \text{Q 5 3}
\end{array}
$$

I. What Happened:

A. The bidding:

In first position I passed. My LHO bid one diamond, which was passed around to me. Because of my shape, I balanced with a double. Before partner had a chance to bid, LHO bids three diamonds, which buys the auction.

The Bidding

N	E	S	W
	pass	1D	pass
pass	double	3D	all pass

B. The play:

Jo lays down the queen of spades.

North (dummy)
♠ 9 5 3
♥ Q 10 5 2
♦ A 7
♣ 8 6 4 2

East (me)
♠ K 8 6 2
♥ A 8 7 4
♦ 9 6
♣ Q 5 3

Dummy had six highs and never opened his mouth. We may have been lucky here to get away with a partial. Declarer takes his ace of spades, plays a diamond to dummy's ace and a club back to his hand. He inserts the jack which loses to partner's king. Declarer then ruffs the spade return, draws the balance of the trumps in two more rounds as I pitch a heart, and lays down the king of hearts. I allow that to win (as partner plays the "3"), but take the heart continuation as partner plays the jack and dummy the queen. Declarer ruffs the next spade and pitches his losing club on the long heart, making five.

C. Results:

We got a two on a top of seven. Not very good.

North-South Pair Number	Contract	Made	Down	East-West Points	East-West Matchpoints
1.	3DS	4		-130	4
2.	3DS	4		-130	4
3. (us)	3DS	5		-150	2
4.	3NTN	3		-400	1
5.	5CS		2	+100	7
6.	4HN	4		-420	0
7.	3DS	4		-130	4
8.	1NTS	2		-120	6

We were the only pair to allow the declarer in diamonds to make five.

North (dummy)
♠ 9 5 3
♥ Q 10 5 2
♦ A 7
♣ 8 6 4 2

West (Jo)
♠ Q J 10 7 4
♥ J 3
♦ 10 5 3
♣ K 10 7

East (me)
♠ K 8 6 2
♥ A 8 7 4
♦ 9 6
♣ Q 5 3

South
♠ A
♥ K 9 6
♦ K Q J 8 4 2
♣ A J 9

II. What Should Have Been:

A. The bidding:

Certainly, from the North-South point of view, North should have found a bid . . . such as one heart. It should not be too difficult for them to find their way to three notrump, with a good chance for success (or even four hearts). In three notrump, after winning the spade lead, South would cash six diamonds, putting the squeeze on both East and West. West would have to find three pitches, such as a club and two spades. East would have to find four. He may pitch a club, a heart and two spades or two hearts and one spade. In any event, three notrump will make. It is a distinct underbid, and may have been very costly for North not to open his mouth. Another question is whether or not West should bid 3 spades on that auction. I feel that it is debatable, but it is probably better and safer to pass. Furthermore, North may then find his way to three notrump or they may reach some other better contract, such as four hearts.

B. The play:

After West wins the club finesse, a small club back will hold the contract to four but is a very tough play to make. The normal play is certainly the spade return. When South plays his king of hearts, and West plays the three, East thinks that West has three hearts and South two. When, however, West plays the jack on the second round, East should then read the position and hold up for one more round. He will then get a club and a heart trick (and hold the contract to four). East erred on this one and gave the declarer an extra trick. Furthermore, he pitched a heart

243

on the third diamond. He should have pitched a spade. Not a very astute defense, if I may be self-destructive.

Lessons:

1. If partner appears to be giving count in a situation, but the play of a later card indicates that the giving of count for one's partner may have been impossible, one should then get a revised count and act accordingly.

2. Responding to a partner's opening bid is mandatory with six card high points (presuming it is not a third hand opener . . . and even then some would consider it mandatory).

41. Cash Out!

Jo is not with us again this week, so I am playing with Artie. Do you remember him from hand number 32? We play a very limited system compared to what Jo and I play.

I. What Happened:

A. The bidding:

In fourth position I pick up my usual nine highs.

East (me)

♠ A K 6 3

♥ 10 6 3

♦ Q 10 6 2

♣ 8 5

South is the dealer and opens with one club. Partner

passes and RHO bids one spade, which keeps me out of
the bidding. LHO then jumps to 3NT, where it remains.

The Bidding

N	E	S	W
		1C	pass
1S	pass	3NT	all pass

B. The play:

Partner is on lead and selects the three of diamonds.

North (dummy)
♠ J 9 8 7 5 4
♥ J 8
♦ J 7 5
♣ K 10

East (me)
♠ A K 6 3
♥ 10 6 3
♦ Q 10 6 2
♣ 8 5

Dummy plays small and I insert the ten, which draws
the ace from declarer. Declarer leads the queen of spades
from his hand, and I duck it. Then he leads a small club
to dummy, and the king wins. I win the small spade from
the dummy with the king as declarer shows out and partner plays the ten (looks like we gave them a trick). I push

back a small diamond which is won by the jack of dummy (gave them another one). I win the jack of spades and declarer pitches the ace of hearts. The only reason he would do that is for a dummy entry when he holds solid hearts, so I return a club, our only hope at this point. Declarer then claims . . . good spades and hearts.

C. Results:

We got a well deserved 1 on the board.

North (dummy)
♠ J 9 8 7 5 4
♥ J 8
♦ J 7 5
♣ K 10

West (partner)
♠ 10 2
♥ 7 5 4 2
♦ 9 4 3
♣ A Q 9 4

East (me)
♠ A K 6 3
♥ 10 6 3
♦ Q 10 6 2
♣ 8 5

South (declarer)
♠ Q
♥ A K Q 9
♦ A K 8
♣ J 7 6 3 2

North-South Pair Number	Contract	Made	Down	East-West Points	East-West Matchpoints
1.	4SN		1	+100	6
2.	3NTS	3		-600	3½
3.	3NTS	4		-630	1
4.	4NTS	4		-630	1
5.	2NTS	2		-120	5
6. (us)	3NTS	4		-630	1
7.	3NTS	3		-600	3½

Five of the seven North-Souths played in game in notrump from the South side. Three made four notrump and two made three notrump. We had several opportunities to hold it to three but failed to take advantage of them.

II. What Should Have Been:

A. The bidding:

I believe that all parties concerned made the right bids. Some may say that South should bid 2NT instead of 3 and some who play weak jump shifts may have opted to bid 2 spades with the North hand. But, on balance, I think that most pairs would have done what the pair in question did. This is one of the very few hands where the play was more important than the bidding.

B. The play:

I believe that West (Artie) did the right thing by not leading a club from four to a tenace, especially in a suit his RHO had bid. He then has a choice of suits. Spades rates to be unfavorable because it was bid to his left. That leaves diamonds and hearts. Some would opt for the four card major and some for the minor. If the major is

248

chosen, perhaps the seven is the card, or the five. If the minor is picked, I believe that the three is the wrong card. It certainly threw off Artie's partner. He should have picked the nine. East, for his part, made a mistake of returning a diamond. Declarer won with the ace on the first round. That cannot be correct unless declarer also holds the king. He gave declarer a free finesse. West made another mistake by not cashing his ace of clubs when he was in with the queen. He should have read the situation with the hearts from the discard of the ace, and at that point cashed out. We could have held it to three right there and picked up at least an average board. Not very good defense.

Lessons:

1. When you see no chance of getting other tricks and you are on defense, cash out.

2. If you have no good lead to make against notrump, pick the least objectionable suit and lead the card which will not mislead partner.

42. Losing Count

Week 42
Board 16
None vulnerable
West Dealer

In the third position I pick up this hand:

East (dummy - me)
♠ 10 8 7
♥ A K
♦ A Q 9 4 3
♣ 10 9 2

I. What Happened:

A. The bidding:

To my surprise, partner opens: 1S. I respond with a two diamond call. Partner bids 2NT and I have a choice: 3NT or 4 spades. My guess is that partner has the black suits well stopped and has queen-third of hearts. Therefore, ruffing a heart in dummy will be useless in four spades. My 10's should also be of value in the black suits. Because of the above and the balance of my hand,

it seems as though 3NT should play as well as 4 spades
and be worth an extra 10 critical points. I bid 3NT.

The Bidding

N	E	S	W
			1S
pass	2D	pass	2NT
pass	3NT	all pass	

B. The play:

I'll describe the hand as partner saw it:

West (declarer - Jo)
♠ K Q J 6 3
♥ Q J 2
♦ 8 5
♣ K J 6

East (dummy - me)
♠ 10 8 7
♥ A K
♦ A Q 9 4 3
♣ 10 9 2

Jo gets the lead of the three of clubs (not a bad lead).
The ace is played by RHO and back comes the eight of
clubs to the jack and queen. Then a heart goes to dummy. Jo leads the ten of spades from dummy which is taken
by LHO's ace. Back comes another heart. Jo then reels
off four more spades, LHO casting off the four of clubs
on the third spade, followed by the ten of hearts and the
five of clubs. RHO pitches two small diamonds. A diamond to the queen holds. Jo then cashes the ace. She then
leads a club to her hand and her queen of hearts is good
for making four. She lost a spade and two clubs.

251

C. Results:

North-South Pair Number	Contract	Made	Down	East-West Points	East-West Matchpoints
1.	4SW	4		+ 620	3½
2.	4SW	4		+ 620	3½
3.	3SW	5		+ 200	1
4.	4SW	4		+ 620	3½
5. (us)	3NTW	4		+ 630	6
6.	4SW	4		+ 620	3½
7.	3NTW		1	-100	0

Note that five spades did make one time. Apparently the diamonds were set up before the queen of clubs was cashed.

The hands were as follows:

North
♠ A 2
♥ 10 8 5
♦ K J 2
♣ Q 7 5 4 3

West (declarer - Jo)
♠ K Q J 6 3
♥ Q J 2
♦ 8 5
♣ K J 6

East (dummy - me)
♠ 10 8 7
♥ A K
♦ A Q 9 4 3
♣ 10 9 2

South
♠ 9 5 4
♥ 9 7 6 4 3
♦ 10 7 6
♣ A 8

In any event, it appears to have been a bid that worked: we got a top.

II. What Should Have Been:

A. The bidding:

Normally, the only lead which holds four spades to four is a club with a club return. Otherwise, the diamonds may set up and five spades will make. However, that does not mean that 3NT is the wrong bid. It worked here and was the case also, you may remember, on hand 5. With balance in the "short hand", and the other suits well stopped (despite an eight card major suit fit), notrump will usually be worth an extra ten points . . . critical in a pair game.

B. The play:

North sure blew it this time. She found the killing lead. Her partner had the ace and came back a club (which she won with the queen). Now dummy had left the ten of clubs and the king was the only card still out. All she had to do was push back one more club. Her ace of spades would have been her entry for the last two clubs and the setting tricks. Why she stopped is a bit of a mystery. Perhaps she lost count. Perhaps she was trying to protect her king of diamonds. What a break for the good guys! As the cards lie, 3NT is doomed with a club lead.

Lessons:

1. When your side has a 5-3 major suit fit, but the short hand has no ruffing power because of balance, and the other suits are well stopped and a dummy reversal is not possible because of weak trumps in dummy, 3NT will often be a better contract in a pair game.

2. It may sound a bit elementary, but keeping track of the number of cards played in a suit (and the number therefore outstanding) will often provide the key to proper defense.

43. Balancing

Week 43
Board 17
None vulnerable
North Dealer

I. What Happened:

A. The bidding:

Another average hand.

```
                              East (me)
                           ♠  K 7
                           ♥  8 7 2
                           ♦  A Q 4 3
                           ♣  9 7 6 4
```

RHO passes, as do I and LHO. Jo Ann bids one heart. Because we play a 1NT forcing, I am rather limited on this hand. I bid two hearts, which buys the contract.

The Bidding

N	E	S	W
			1H
pass	pass	pass	1H
pass	2H	all pass	

B. The play:

Jo's LHO leads the king of clubs and I spread my hand ... I have nine points and I promised her 8-9 by my direct raise. I'll now describe the hand as she saw it:

West (declarer - Jo)	East (dummy)
♠ A 6 4	♠ K 7
♥ K 9 6 4 3	♥ 8 7 2
♦ 6 5	♦ A Q 4 3
♣ A 5 3	♣ 9 7 6 4

Jo takes the ace on the first trick, as South plays the ten. She next leads the four of spades to the king and a spade back to her hand (LHO drops the jack). She then ruffs a spade in dummy. Next, she leads the six of clubs from dummy and lets it ride to the eight of LHO. LHO then leads the ten of diamonds, which Jo wins with the ace. Back comes another club, which RHO ruffs. RHO then leads the ace of hearts and LHO delivers the eight of diamonds (OOPS), which becomes a penalty card, and then he follows with the ten of hearts. RHO then cashes the king of diamonds. Then he leads the seven of diamonds, which is ruffed by Jo. She then leads a heart to the queen of her LHO, and ruffs the return of the queen of clubs. Her king of hearts provides the last trick,

256

making 2 for a plus 110.

Let's take a look at all four hands:

北

North
- ♠ J 9 2
- ♥ Q J 10
- ♦ J 10 8
- ♣ K Q J 8

West	East
♠ A 6 4	♠ K 7
♥ K 9 6 4 3	♥ 8 7 2
♦ 6 5	♦ A Q 4 3
♣ A 5 3	♣ 9 7 6 4

South
- ♠ Q 10 8 5 3
- ♥ A 5
- ♦ K 9 7 2
- ♣ 10 2

C. Results:

North-South Pair Number	Contract	Made	Down	East-West Points	East-West Matchpoints
1.	2SS	2		-110	½
2.	3CN		1	+50	2½
3.	2HW	2		+110	4½
4. (us)	2HW	2		+110	4½
5.	2NTN		1	+50	2½
6.	2SN	2		-110	½

We got a tie for top on this simple hand. Why?

II. What Should Have Been:

A. The bidding:

It is quite obvious that if North-South refuse to let East-West buy the contract for two hearts and instead bid two spades, they will get a good board. When the opponents agree on a suit and pass at the two level, chances are the points are evenly distributed between the two sides. It makes little sense, therefore, to let the opponents name the trump suit . . . at least force them one level higher. Here we have a classic case. North should have doubled in the pass out position and South would have bid two spades. No matter what West did then, North-South would have gotten a good board. They controlled the master suit.

That brings us to another point. Should you open the bidding in 4th position without control of the master suit, and less than a full opener, one rule of thumb is that if your high cards and the number of spades you hold total less than 15, you should not open. Jo had 11 highs and 3 spades. She fell short. Despite the 2½ quick tricks, she did not control the master suit, and, with proper bidding by North-South, she would end up on the short end of the stick on average. The bid she made is not outlandish, but, on balance, not a matchpoint bid. Here it worked. We were lucky.

B. The play:

It is very hard to see how Jo could have made an over-trick. I think I'll let you slide on this one Jo . . . after all, you just took the heat despite getting us a top board.

Lessons:

1. When the opponents agree on a suit, don't let them buy the contract on the two level (especially with equal vulnerability or when you are not and they are). Double or bid in the pass out position.

2. Don't open in fourth position unless you have a total of 15 points (HCP's + the number of spades in your hand).

3. Do not assume that you are immune from criticism when you get a top on a board.

44. Place The Contract

Week 44
Board 18
North-South vulnerable
East Dealer

This week we have a seven table game and are facing two males who have not played together before, to my knowledge.

I. What Happened:

A. The bidding:

As East and dealer I pick up these cards:

East
♠ A 7
♥ Q J 8 4
♦ Q J 7
♣ Q J 4 2

I open up one club. My LHO bids one spade. Partner passes and RHO bids two diamonds. LHO bids two spades. RHO jumps to four diamonds which is carried back to four spades by LHO. All pass.

N	E	S	W
—	1C	1S	pass
2D	pass	2S	pass
4D	pass	4S	all pass

B. The play:

Partner finds the lead of the six of clubs as dummy is spread.

North (dummy)

♠ 9 6
♥ K 9 7
♦ A K 10 8 6 5 3
♣ 8

East (me)

♠ A 7
♥ Q J 8 4
♦ Q J 7
♣ Q J 4 2

LHO takes my jack with his ace. He then ruffs a club. Back comes a heart to his ace and another club ruff. He then plays the ace of diamonds followed by the king (on which he pitches a club). Next is the king of hearts and a heart ruff in hand. He then leads out his king of spades . . . and all I get is my ace, making six.

That can't be very good. Right again. It's not. A four-

261

way tie for bottom.

North-South Pair Number	Contract	Made	Down	East-West Points	East-West Matchpoints
1.	3DN	5		-150	6
2.	5DN	5		-600	4
3.	4SS	6		-680	1½
4.	3SS	6		-230	5
5. (us)	4SS	6		-680	1½
6.	4SS	6		-680	1½
7.	4SS	6		-680	1½

Where did we err?

North (dummy)
- ♠ 9 6
- ♥ K 9 7
- ♦ A K 10 8 6 5 3
- ♣ 8

West (Jo)
- ♠ 8 3 2
- ♥ 10 5 3 2
- ♦ 4 2
- ♣ K 9 6 5

East (me)
- ♠ A 7
- ♥ Q J 8 4
- ♦ Q J 7
- ♣ Q J 4 2

South (declarer)
- ♠ K Q J 10 5 4
- ♥ A 6
- ♦ 9
- ♣ A 10 7 3

The name of the game was reaching game in spades. We had very little control on this hand.

II. What Should Have Been:

A. The bidding:

Obviously, those who failed to reach game in spades got a bad board. We were the unlucky opponents of those who did. South made a poor bid by only bidding two spades at his second call. He might have been passed by a partner who may have have seen no game in the offing opposite a partner with five spades and ten points. He almost blew it. But, his partner rescued him with his bid of four diamonds. In my opinion, South should have jumped right to four spades after his partner's free bid at the two level. His partner shows ten points, and South has a self-sufficient spade suit. He can play in game opposite a ten point hand (which figures to be in diamonds and hearts). After his partner shows his points by his bid, South should place the contract. I should note that my partner (Jo Ann) feels that a re-bid of three spades is more appropriate. I believe that the experts would be divided on this. Few, I imagine, would think a bid of two spades correct. When South bids three spades or four spades, North should allow a game in spades to be bid. He should not pull to diamonds, as he has two spades (which is adequate support).

B. The play:

There was nothing unusual here. Of course, a spade lead could hold it to four, but a spade lead is hardly called

263

for. The name of the game was reaching game in spades.

Lessons:

1. When you know that your side has the points for game and a suit to play it in, putting the contract where it belongs (especially when your side is the overcalling side) will often avoid the embarrassment of being passed out short of game. Take the bull by the horns.

2. Unless you are totally broke in your partner's re-bid major suit, it is often better to play in that major rather than in your minor.

45. Set Up The Jack

Week 45
Board 19
East-West vulnerable
South Dealer

I. What Happened:

  A. The bidding:

In a 7½ table evening, we face a married couple. I have more than my share of points, though nothing to write home about.

East (me)
♠ K J 5 2
♥ A 8 6 3
♦ A 3
♣ 10 9 7

South passes and my partner opens with a call of one club. RHO overcalls one spade. Among my options is one that I select . . . 3NT. I could have negative doubled, but my hand looks like it should play nicely in notrump. And, I have the opportunity to conceal the heart suit. I certainly don't want to stop in less than game.

The Bidding

N	E	S	W
		pass	1C
1S	3NT	all pass	

B. The play:

I get the expected spade lead (but the unexpected pleasure of the queen of spades). RHO lets it ride, and I win.

West (dummy - Jo)
♠ 9 8
♥ Q J 10
♦ J 10 7 2
♣ A K Q 3

East (declarer - me)
♠ K J 5 2
♥ A 8 6 3
♦ A 3
♣ 10 9 7

I count my tricks and see two spades (if the ace is onside . . . which I expect it to be), three hearts, one diamond and three clubs. The question is: should I first hook the heart, play for the 3-3 club fit, set up my jack of spades, or hook the club (or even play on diamonds). I elect to first hook the heart. I enter dummy with a club and lead the queen of hearts. In any event, it rides to the king of LHO. I now have nine tricks in the bag if I can set up my jack of spades. LHO returns a diamond to the jack, king and my ace. I lead a heart to dummy, cash the other heart and then play a spade. RHO grabs her ace and leads back a club. I play my nine, covered by the jack and won by the dummy. This is what remains:

Dummy	Declarer
♠	♠ J 5
♥	♥ A
♦ 10 7 2	♦ 3
♣ Q 3	♣ 10

I have won six tricks and am on dummy. I have to play to make, so I abandon the hope of a 3-3 club fit and lead away from the good queen of clubs to my ten. I cash the spade and the heart and end up bagging nine tricks. Looks easy, right? Not necessarily.

C. Results:

Another top. We seem to be improving.

North
♠ A 10 7 6 4 3
♥ 7 5
♦ K 9 5
♣ 5 2

West (dummy - Jo)
♠ 9 8
♥ Q J 10
♦ J 10 7 2
♣ A K Q 3

East (declarer - me)
♠ K J 5 2
♥ A 8 6 3
♦ A 3
♣ 10 9 7

South
♠ Q
♥ K 9 4 2
♦ Q 8 6 4
♣ J 8 6 4

North-South Pair Number	Contract	Made	Down	East-West Points	East-West Matchpoints
1.	2HE	2		+ 110	3½
2.	1NTE	3		+ 150	5
3.	3CW	3		+ 110	3½
4.	3NTE		1	-100	1½
5. (us)	3NTE	3		+ 600	6
6.	3NTW		1	-100	1½
7.	3NTE		2	-200	0

It is a little hard to understand, but only four of the seven pairs reached game. And, of the four who did (all playing in notrump), we were the only ones who made it.

II. What Should Have Been:

A. The bidding:

It would, indeed, be most unusual for me to stop short of game after my partner opens and my RHO indicated strength in spades when I have the points and holding that I do. By bidding 3NT directly, I tell partner I can play opposite 13 points and have a probable double stop in the suit of the overcaller. My guess is also that K-J-fourth would be better for notrump than for a suit . . . and requires one less trick. Furthermore, I have nice holdings in the off suits. When you think you know where the contract should be and can at the same time describe your hand to partner, place the contract (we also saw this in last week's hand).

B. The play:

It was also the play of the hand which got us the good board, in this case. When the tricks are there, or you think that they are, timing becomes the critical factor. It was in this case. It was very important for East to set up the spade jack after the heart finesse lost instead of using some other method of play.

The possibility of a 3-3 club break would always be there. On the lead of the second spade, South pitched a diamond. Remember, East had first cashed the two remaining hearts in dummy. East should have only cashed one of them, preserving the other for communication. Then, he has South in a squeeze on the second spade lead at trick six. South has to protect three suits. If he then pitches the heart, the ten of hearts could be overtaken and declarer's long heart made into the ninth trick. If he pitched a minor, dummy's long club or diamond would have been good. When East had cashed the two hearts in dummy, South could have avoided a trap by pitching a heart. East had lost communication. Then, if North had led a diamond to South's queen, and South returned a diamond to West's ten, South's long club and extra diamond would have been good and the contract defeated. The mistake made by East was cashing the third heart. But, as South defended and North returned a club, it ended up costing nothing.

Then, when in dummy, declarer had to abandon the queen of clubs to return to his good ace of hearts and jack of spades.

Lessons:

1. Planning the timing of the hand is something which should be done before the first card is played and should be updated continuously as the hand progresses.

2. If you have the opportunity to place the contract and let your partner know (by so doing) what your holding is, seize the chance and place the contract.

3. When declarer, it is obviously important to keep communication in mind (constantly) between dummy and declarer.

46. A Series Of Overbids

Week 46
Board 20
Both vulnerable
West Dealer

This week Jo is on vacation, but my brother Lloyd is in visiting from Miami, anyhow. Lloyd and I play basically the same system as Jo and I, so don't worry about getting confused any more than you are. Lloyd and I are playing against a mother-son combo tonight. They are inexperienced and, as a result, unpredictable, but they show a lot of promise . . . they are both beginning to study the game, which is rare in these parts.

I. What Happened:

A. The bidding:

As East I pick up a heart suit and nothing else:

East (me)

♠ 9 8 6
♥ A K Q 6 3
♦ 4 3
♣ 9 5 4

Partner is the dealer and passes. So does RHO and so do I. LHO bids one spade, partner doubles and RHO bids two diamonds. I have a choice of two hearts and three hearts. However, I select two hearts in hopes of buying it here. South supports diamonds at the three level and partner, surprisingly, comes in with three hearts. RHO is not to be denied, however, as he comes in with three spades, which LHO increases to four. An awful lot of bidding, it seems to me.

The Bidding

N	E	S	W
			pass
pass	pass	1S	double
2D	2H	3D	3H
3S	pass	4S	all pass

B. The play:

Partner leads the jack of hearts as dummy comes down.

North (dummy)
- ♠ J 7 4
- ♥ 9 7 4
- ♦ K Q J 8 7
- ♣ Q 8

East (me)
- ♠ 9 8 6
- ♥ A K Q 6 3
- ♦ 4 3
- ♣ 9 5 4

Dummy plays low and I overtake the jack with the queen but LHO ruffs. LHO then leads a small spade toward the jack and partner wins the king. He continues with the two of hearts which is also ruffed by LHO. LHO then produces a small spade which is won by partner's queen. A third heart follows, ruffed with the ace. Back comes a club to partner's ace. Partner continues with a club and church is out. Won by the queen in dummy and the jack of spades drew my last trump. The diamonds are good as declarer has the ace-third, making four. If partner had just continued with hearts one more time, we would have set the contract and my last spade would have been good (to say nothing of additional hearts).

C. Results:

Not a very good board . . . a one on a top of six. Did we err or were we fixed? Let's take a look at the hands and the results:

North
♠ J 7 4
♥ 9 7 4
♦ K Q J 8 7
♣ Q 8

West (partner)
♠ K Q
♥ J 10 8 5 2
♦ 9 6 5
♣ A J 2

East (me)
♠ 9 8 6
♥ A K Q 6 3
♦ 4 3
♣ 9 5 4

South
♠ A 10 5 3 2
♥
♦ A 10 2
♣ K 10 7 6 3

North-South Pair Number	Contract	Made	Down	East-West Points	East-West Matchpoints
1.	3SS	4		-170	3½
2.	3HW	3		+140	6
3. (us)	4SS	4		-620	1
4.	2SS	3		-140	5
5.	2SS	5		-200	2
6.	4SS	5		-650	0
7.	3SS	4		-170	3½

Only two of the North-South teams got to game. We were fixed to that extent. It seems as though it was typical for the contract to make four spades. Let's take a look at what should have been.

II. What Should Have Been:

A. The bidding:

After the opening of one spade (following three passes), the double by West (vulnerable) is questionable. He has perhaps nine working points. I would say a pass is in order. In any event, North stretches by bidding two diamonds and later returning to spades. Some would say a direct call of two spades is more appropriate with nine highs. Probably South would then pass and they would end up in the normal contract of two spades. But, North stretched. South came back with diamond support after the free intervention by East with a call of two hearts. I believe the diamond bid is correct. Then, West, after overbidding by the double, makes another bid opposite the passed hand and repeats his support for hearts by raising the suit he essentially bid himself. That is a no-no.

He should pass three diamonds. Then, following a return to three spades, should that have occurred, South would have the decision to make about the trip to the four level. Basically, a series of overbids led to our demise.

B. The play:

With proper defense, the hand might be defeated. If declarer tries two hooks in spades, which seems normal, and loses both, in addition to the ace of clubs, she has a problem drawing trumps if forced with hearts. Suppose she ruffs the first heart and then leads a club for the first hook. If the queen wins, she loses to the trump king. A heart continuation and ruff. Then, a diamond to the king and another hook to the ten and queen. Another heart (the third). Then declarer is dead. She is out of trumps and East has one behind dummy's jack. Her best chance is to play ace and a spade, hoping to catch an honor-doubleton. This is the winning line.

But, as she played it, the hand has trouble with proper defense. If only West had continued hearts one more time. How was he to know that his partner had another trump. First, South did not re-bid the suit (thereby probably indicating only five). Second, the eight spot was missing. Third, Jo and I, but not Lloyd and I, play a trump echo. High-low in trumps indicates the presence of a third trump. But we were not playing that system, so West had to presume that South would have re-bid a six-card suit. We missed the chance to take advantage of the overbids.

Lessons:

1. Counting on a hand is very important.

2. Repeating your statement (as did West) is negative in that you are taking a chance on misleading partner and getting doubled.

3. Sophisticated defense techniques pay off . . . the more systems, the more accurate the defense (within limits).

47. Lead Of The Ace

Week 47
Board 21
North-South vulnerable
North Dealer

With only a few weeks to go, I pick up this hand in second position:

East
♠ Q 9 8 2
♥ K 6 2
♦ 10 9 5 4 3 2
♣

I. What Happened:

A. The bidding:

My RHO opens with a 1NT call (16-18). I decide (non-vulnerable) to muddy the waters a little with an overcall of two diamonds. South passes, as does partner. RHO decides that she was not descriptive enough with her 1NT

bid, so she sticks in a 3 club bid, which is passed around
to my partner's call of 3D. That, then, is passed to South
who injects a call of four clubs. Partner doubles, but I
pull it to four diamonds because of my weakness defen-
sively. That is passed around to North who doubles, ending the auction . . . a spirited one.

The Bidding

N	E	S	W
1NT	2D	pass	pass
3C	pass	pass	3D
pass	pass	4C	double
pass	4D	pass	pass
double all pass			

B. The play:

My LHO is on lead and finds the perfect lead of the
ace of clubs. Jo spreads her hand and has a bit more than
I expected, although she had to have a nice hand, judg-
ing from the bidding.

West (dummy - Jo)	East
♠ K J 10 7	♠ Q 9 8 2
♥ Q 10 5 3	♥ K 6 2
♦ A J 7	♦ 10 9 5 4 3 2
♣ K 7	♣

She has 14 highs, including a well-placed king of clubs. In any event, I ruff the club lead, to the obvious dismay of North. I then lead the ten of diamonds and forsake the finesse when it is not covered, noting with interest and delight the fall of the king from RHO. She must have the king-queen (she opened 1NT). She would not have opened 1NT with a singleton and would not otherwise drop the king. I therefore lead small from dummy's J-X, and am rewarded with the fall of the queen. She then cashes the ace of hearts, hoping her partner has the king. I then am able to claim, giving up the ace of spades, making four doubled. That ought to be a top.

C. Results:

Not quite a top, but close.

North
- ♠ A 6 3
- ♥ A 7
- ♦ K Q
- ♣ Q J 10 9 8 5

West (dummy - Jo)
- ♠ K J 10 7
- ♥ Q 10 5 3
- ♦ A J 7
- ♣ K 7

East (declarer - me)
- ♠ Q 9 8 2
- ♥ K 6 2
- ♦ 10 9 5 4 3 2
- ♣

South
- ♠ 5 4
- ♥ J 9 8 4
- ♦ 8 6
- ♣ A 6 4 3 2

North-South Pair Number	Contract	Made	Down	East-West Points	East-West Matchpoints
1.	4DE*	4		+ 510	5½
2. (us)	4DE*	4		+ 510	5½
3.	4DE	4		+ 130	3
4.	3CN	3		-110	0
5.	5DE*		1	-100	1
6.	5CN*		1	+ 200	4
7.	4CN		1	+ 100	2

There was apparently a lot of bidding competition on this hand. In retrospect, I suppose the 1NT opener hurt North in that South could have more easily come in with support if North had opened one club instead, which is probably what most did.

II. What Should Have Been:

   A. The bidding:

   I think that North takes quite a chance, vulnerable with a 1NT opener. A one club opener is more descriptive and certainly less likely to lead to calamity. Besides, he has no tenace to protect by being declarer. For East's part, non-vul against vul, he has little to lose by sticking in his bid (with the playing strength of his hand). He further takes away Stayman and transfers. Especially against weak opponents who don't play Lebensohl, it can be very effective intervention. Other than that, North's double may be a bit risky. For sure, she can only see three tricks, and her partner has indicated little (except for clubs, which cannot be counted on to produce a trick). She is better off passing quietly along the way. For doing so, she would at least salvage an average board.

   B. The play:

   I try to make it a practice never to lead out the ace of a suit both my partner and I have bid. It seems that when I do (very often), my RHO holds the king and I fail to trap it. Perhaps another lead would have been more productive. Perhaps that is double dummy in this case, but in general it seems to work best to find another lead.

Without the lead of the ace of clubs, declarer would have had to play the hearts just right or he would have gone down. He would have had to lead the king and finesse the ten. In any other fashion the contract would not have made.

Lessons:

1. It is often a good idea not to lead out the ace of a suit both you and your partner have bid, especially if there is reason to expect that the king might be on your right (other things being equal). The lead of a king or queen in the supported suit bears no such danger.

2. When non-vulnerable against vulnerable opponents who have opened the bidding with 1NT (if you have an offensive hand), it is not only not risky but is often a good move to interfere in that it deprives the opponents of the use of several gadgets they might use in response to a notrump opener. It further paves the way for a possible sacrifice.

48. Issue An Invitation

Week 48
Board 22
East-West vulnerable
East Dealer

Talk about boring hands. This is one, illustrative of our club's level of expertise.

I. What Happened:

A. The bidding:

Against a former partner of mine and his new and inexperienced partner, we find ourselves seated in this 8½ table evening.

My hand lacks excitement:

East
♠ 8 4 3 2
♥ 7 4
♦ 4 3 2
♣ Q J 6 4

I pass, of course. My left hand opponent bids one heart.

Partner passes. RHO bids two hearts. I pass and LHO bids four, after which all pass.

The Bidding

N	E	S	W
	pass	1H	pass
2H	pass	4H	all pass

B. The play:

Partner is on lead. She finds the seven of spades.

North (dummy)
♠ K 9 6
♥ 10 6 3 2
♦ Q 8 6
♣ A 7 2

East (me)
♠ 8 4 3 2
♥ 7 4
♦ 4 3 2
♣ Q J 6 4

Declarer wins the king in dummy and leads a small heart to her nine and partner's ace. Partner persists with the five of spades which declarer wins in hand with the queen. She then cashes the ace of spades, believe it or not, all following. A club to the ace and a heart back to her hand draws the rest of the trumps. She then leads a diamond to her dummy's queen, but partner pops up with the king. Partner cashes the king of clubs, and declarer claims, making four.

C. Results:

We got a "1."

North (dummy)
♠ K 9 6
♥ 10 6 3 2
♦ Q 8 6
♣ A 7 2

<table>
<tr><td>West (Jo)</td><td>East</td></tr>
<tr><td>♠ 10 7 5</td><td>♠ 8 4 3 2</td></tr>
<tr><td>♥ A 8</td><td>♥ 7 4</td></tr>
<tr><td>♦ K J 10 7</td><td>♦ 4 3 2</td></tr>
<tr><td>♣ K 10 9 3</td><td>♣ Q J 6 4</td></tr>
</table>

South (declarer)
♠ A Q J
♥ K Q J 9 5
♦ A 9 5
♣ 8 5

North-South Pair Number	Contract	Made	Down	East-West Points	East-West Matchpoints
1.	3HS	4		-170	4
2.	2HS	4		-170	4
3.	4HS		1	+50	6½
4.	4HS	4		-420	1
5.	5HS		1	+50	6½
6. (us)	4HS	4		-420	1
7.	4HS	4		-420	1
8.	2HS	4		-170	4

Three pairs failed to get to game. Now that hurts! One pair made it to five . . . And, one pair managed to go down . . . somehow. How one pair went down is a bit of a mystery. We just happened to play against a pair that bid and made a very normal game.

II. What Should Have Been:

A. The bidding:

North and South have 26 highs between them and a nine card major suit fit. To not find your way to game under those conditions demeans the game of Bridge. Even in standard bidding, South would, in response to a raise of one heart, raise to "3" to see if North had a maximum, which he does. To not explore by bidding 3 means that South would not play game in hearts with less than 28 points in the combined hands. And North, if raised to "3", must not have considered his 10 points or 9 points a maximum. I have difficulty understanding. Jo and I, of course, would have no trouble with the hand. We play the forcing notrump. A direct raise to 2 hearts would show 8-9 points, and a raise to 3 would show 10-12 with 4 pieces. She could do either and I would place the contract in four hearts. The point is, though, that the South hand certainly merits an invitation to game, and three couples did not issue that invitation or did not accept it. With a single direct raise, however, looking for slam is out of the question . . . which is what one pair did.

B. The play:

The only comment is that declarer should have gotten

the children off the street before playing on one of the other suits, of course.

Lessons:

1. When you have a hand which merits an invitation opposite a direct raise to the 2 level of your major suit opener (a hand with 16-18 points), you should issue such an invitation. And, when given one, accept it if your hand is at the top half of the possible holdings and decline if it is in the bottom half, other things being equal.

2. Generally, if you open at less than the 2 level (have fewer than 23 or so points including distribution) and get a direct 1 level raise of your major suit opener, you are too weak to explore for slam.

49. Risky Business

Week 49
Board 23
Both vulnerable
South Dealer

This week Jo is gone, so Bucky and I are playing again. We are playing against two gentlemen.

I. What Happened:

A. The bidding:

In fourth position I pick up the following:

East
♠ 8 6
♥ K Q J 8 7
♦ 7 4 3
♣ K Q 10

But, after two passes, RHO opens 1NT. Should I bid 2 hearts (we play natural over notrump) or should I pass and hope they end up playing in notrump, despite my shortness in spades? I choose to pass. As it turns out, 1NT is passed out, so I get to lead. I wonder what I'll lead. I manage to find the lead of the king of hearts as dummy comes down.

East (me)
♠ 8 6
♥ K Q J 8 7
♦ 7 4 3
♣ K Q 10

South (dummy)
♠ 9 5 4 2
♥ 6 5
♦ A 10 6
♣ 9 7 6 4

B. The play:

The king of hearts holds, as partner contributes the "3" and declarer the 2. That means that partner either has 3 of them or has a singleton, which is unlikely. I continue with the queen, which declarer wins. He then leads the ten of spades to partner's ace. Partner then finds the killing return of the 10 of hearts. Should I overtake? I know that that is the last heart (except for declarer's). But, I would like a club switch. I decide to overtake (lead out the rest of the hearts) and lead the king of clubs. Declarer wins, rattling off three more spades. Then, he leads to the ace of diamonds in dummy and a diamond back to his hand. Partner wins the king and returns a club to set the contract one trick. We won four hearts, a spade, a diamond and a club.

C. Results:

North (declarer)
- ♠ K Q J 10
- ♥ A 9 2
- ♦ Q 9 5 2
- ♣ A J

West (partner - Bucky)
- ♠ A 7 3
- ♥ 10 4 3
- ♦ K J 8
- ♣ 8 5 3 2

East (me)
- ♠ 8 6
- ♥ K Q J 8 7
- ♦ 7 4 3
- ♣ K Q 10

South (dummy)
- ♠ 9 5 4 2
- ♥ 6 5
- ♦ A 10 6
- ♣ 9 7 6 4

North-South Pair Number	Contract	Made	Down	East-West Points	East-West Matchpoints
1.	2HE	2		+ 110	6
2.	1NTN		1	+ 100	3½
3.	1NTN		1	+ 100	3½
4.	1NTN	2		-120	0
5.	1NTN		1	+ 100	3½
6. (us)	1NTN		1	+ 100	3½
7.	2HE		1	-100	1

Let's look at the results. Five of the East players let North buy the contract and set it four of the five times.

Two bid two hearts and one made it. With proper defense (or maybe lucky defense), it can be set. But normally East rates to lose two diamonds, one spade, one heart and one club. In any event, we got an above average board, so I'm satisfied.

II. What Should Have Been:

A. The bidding:

From East's perspective, North-South have between 29 and 17 points (remember that South and West passed originally). If we figure the average of 23, that means that West has about 6 points (he actually had 8). That means that if East bids, he may, vulnerable, be trying to make 2 hearts with 17 points. The odds may not favor that. If he goes down one, he gets a worse board than if he simply lets North-South make one notrump. Furthermore, if South has more than the average number of points, he could crack any intervention. I believe that East is taking a chance intervening. Against weak opponents, play for an average and let them make the mistakes. It is true that two hearts may make, but then East got lucky finding West with the hand he had and his honors favorably placed. If North-South ended up in spades, a heart lead might be found in any event.

B. The play:

North should have held up until the third round in hearts, to sever the communications between East and West. It may not have made any difference on the actual hand, but could hardly have hurt declarer.

291

Lessons:

1. Overcalling a notrump when you are vulnerable is risky business. What is needed to do that is controls, a strong suit, and the lack of balance (unless, of course, you have a strong hand).

2. Not overcalling a notrump opener when you do have a strong suit sometimes pays off when you have the lead and you expect them to be playing in notrump.

3. If, against non-experts, you have a choice of bids, and have a tough time deciding which to make, pick the one which is not risky.

50. Don't Touch That Suit

Week 50
Board 24
None vulnerable
West Dealer

An opening hand. I'll be.

```
                              East (me)
                              ♠ Q 2
                              ♥ A 10 9 3
                              ♦ A K J 5
                              ♣ 10 9 2
```

I. What Happened:

A. The bidding:

I don't get the chance to open the bidding, because partner opens with one club. I respond one heart (bidding my major first). Partner bids one spade (not a reverse, showing 13-15 points) and I place the contract at 3NT. Our opponents were silent.

The Bidding

N	E	S	W
			1C
pass	1H	pass	1S
pass	3NT	all pass	

B. The play:

I get the lead of the two of hearts, as partner spreads out just what she promised:

♠

West (dummy - Jo)
♠ J 8 6 3
♥ K J
♦ Q 8 2
♣ A K 8 4

East (declarer - me)
♠ Q 2
♥ A 10 9 3
♦ A K J 5
♣ 10 9 2

The jack wins the first trick, and I have a chance for ten tricks, I see. If the club honors are divided (a 75% chance), I will make ten. I then play the queen of diamonds and one back to my hand. Then I lead the ten of clubs, intending to let it ride. But, LHO covers with the jack. It is then a simple matter to win the trick and play a low club to my nine (giving up the queen). A heart comes back to the king. I then cash my diamonds, the ace of hearts, and then go to the board for the good clubs, making four. Nothing tough here.

C. Results:

We tied for top. Why would you expect that we did?

North-South Pair Number	Contract	Made	Down	East-West Points	East-West Matchpoints
1.	3NTW	3		+ 400	3
2.	3NTW	4		+ 430	5½
3.	3NTW	3		+ 400	3
4.	3NTW	3		+ 400	3
5.	3NTW		1	-50	½
6. (us)	3NTE	4		+ 430	5½
7.	4HE		1	-50	½

Well, we were the only pair to play it from the East position.

```
                        North
                      ♠ K 9 5 4
                      ♥ 8 4
                      ♦ 9 6 4
                      ♣ Q 6 5 3

West (dummy - Jo)              East (declarer - me)
♠ J 8 6 3                      ♠ Q 2
♥ K J                          ♥ A 10 9 3
♦ Q 8 2                        ♦ A K J 5
♣ A K 8 4                      ♣ 10 9 2

                        South
                      ♠ A 10 7
                      ♥ Q 7 6 5 2
                      ♦ 10 7 3
                      ♣ J 7
```

Why did 80% of the West declarers make less than 4?

II. What Should Have Been:

A. The bidding:

After the normal opening of one club, East has the option of one diamond or one heart. I prefer the major suit response because you get more for a major suit game, and the lack of a major suit response gives partner a clue (immediate) as to my hand and where the contract belongs. Partner should then re-bid (if it won't show a reverse by partnership agreement) 1 spade or 1NT if it will. If East is 4-4 in the majors, the re-bid of 1 spade will uncover a 4-4 fit in spades. Then, East should place the contract . . . as he knows his partner's values and distribution, within limits. Perhaps most of the West players just re-bid 1NT following a diamond or heart response. They never would have found that 4-4 spade fit, if it did exist. Does that mean that the reason we got a good board is just because of the side of the table from which it was played?

B. The play:

If West is the declarer, the normal opening lead would be a spade (remember West opened one club and spades were probably unmentioned). Declarer should play low from dummy (which guarantees him one trick). Let's suppose that South wins and returns a spade which is won by North. If he then continues spades, West is on lead with the jack. Now, how should West proceed?

He should count his tricks — one spade, two hearts,

four diamonds, and two clubs . . . he has his nine in the bag. Where can he find a tenth . . . clubs or hearts? With clubs he would have to give up a trick (unless the Q-J are doubleton). Then he would also lose a spade, probably. With his heart holding, the best approach is to attack hearts and try to win three tricks there. Now North led a spade, which seems to mean he has four. East has shown three. Therefore, hooking the heart toward the South hand (letting the jack ride after playing the king) will leave South no way to get back to the North hand for the cashing of the spade. If it loses, West still has ten tricks (one spade, A-K-10 of hearts, four diamonds and two clubs). It seems to be as simple as that.

Apparently, it was not. The answer must lie in the play of the spades. Even with the heart hook, declarer has only three hearts, four diamonds and two clubs. He must never have gotten a spade trick. He must have played the queen to trick one or may have broken the suit himself. Either approach is the wrong play. Let them break the suit and play the first honor.

Lessons:

1. In deciding which way to hook, thinking in terms of which opponent you don't want to be in the lead should affect your decision, other things being equal.

2. When you become declarer, one of the first things you should do is to count your tricks and then see if there is any safe way to make one more.

3. If you hold the Q-J bare in a suit (split honors) when playing notrump, don't touch the suit. And when it is played, don't play an honor to the first trick (unless they haven't) to guarantee yourself one trick.

51. Off The Hook

Week 51
Board 25
East-West vulnerable
North Dealer

Once again my brother, Lloyd, is in visiting from Miami. We face a pair of women we have faced before.

I. What Happened:

A. The bidding:

RHO is the dealer and she passes. I have no bid with the following:

> East (me)
> ♠ 9 5
> ♥ J 6 4
> ♦ K 9 8 5
> ♣ K Q 8 4

My LHO opens the bidding with a call of one club. Partner overcalls with one heart and RHO sticks in a one spade call. With nine highs and three hearts, I can afford to raise Lloyd's hearts to the two level, which I do. LHO, however, comes in with a two spade bid. Now it is Lloyd's turn again. He makes the surprising call of four hearts, vulnerable. North steals the bid with a four-spade call. Should I double? I do, to prevent Lloyd from taking any further action.

The Bidding

N	E	S	W
pass	pass	1C	1H
1S	2H	2S	4H
4S	double	all pass	

B. The play:

I'm on lead and pick the four of hearts. Dummy is spread (a light opener):

South (dummy)

East (me)
♠ 9 5
♥ J 6 4
♦ K 9 8 5
♣ K Q 8 4

South (dummy)
♠ A 8 7
♥ Q 8
♦ J 2
♣ A 10 7 6 5 3

Declarer plays the queen from dummy, and Lloyd takes the ace and returns a heart into the arms of declarer's king. Two rounds of trumps are drawn, all following. Then, a club to the ace and a club back to my queen, partner pitching a heart on the second round. We need two diamond tricks to set the contract, so I play a low diamond to Lloyd's ace and he comes back to my king, for down one. It looks as though we would have lost two spades, a club and a heart in four hearts, for also down one. I'm glad we were defending.

C. Results:

A top. How in the world did that happen? First, look at all four hands:

North (declarer)
- ♠ K Q 10 6 4 2
- ♥ K 7
- ♦ 10 6 4
- ♣ 9 2

West (Lloyd)
- ♠ J 3
- ♥ A 10 9 5 3 2
- ♦ A Q 7 3
- ♣ J

East (me)
- ♠ 9 5
- ♥ J 6 4
- ♦ K 9 8 5
- ♣ K Q 8 4

South (dummy)
- ♠ A 8 7
- ♥ Q 8
- ♦ J 2
- ♣ A 10 7 6 5 3

North-South Pair Number	Contract	Made	Down	East-West Points	East-West Matchpoints
1.	3SN	3		-140	½
2.	4HW		1	-100	2½
3.	4SN		1	+50	4½
4. (us)	4SN*		1	+100	6
5.	4SN		1	+50	4½
6.	3SN	3		-140	½
7.	4HW		1	-100	2½

301

It appears that the double was only worth one point. Had they made, we would have had a bottom. But, the double may have served the function of giving partner notice that I want to defend on the hand, rather than buy the contract at the five level, if he had that intention.

II. What Should Have Been:

A. The bidding:

Looking at Lloyd's hand (opposite a passed hand), it hardly seems logical to bid to the four level vulnerable. He has a miserable spade holding and a probable club loser, to say nothing of missing spots in hearts (and diamonds). When I give him a single weak raise, he should be very cautious. Although it is true that if East holds that magic nine points game will make, it is not the percentage thing to do. It turns out that North bit the hook, getting Lloyd off of it, but he was very lucky. In Lloyd's position, I would discount the two jacks, giving him basically 10 working points. They appear to be well placed, and a raise, vulnerable to the three level, would indicate that. But, bidding four is a bit much.

B. The play:

No comment is necessary here.

Lessons:

1. When you voluntarily bid game and the opponents overbid you, in most cases (especially with your side

vulnerable and the opponents' not) either bidding on or doubling them is automatic.

2. When you don't want your partner to continue bidding, doubling will often prevent him from doing that, although the gain in matchpoints is not very great and may be risky.

52. How Very Fitting

Week 52
Board 26
Both vulnerable
East Dealer

For our final hand of this series, I pick something which could not be more fitting: a sub-average hand . . . and an apparently boring one at that. I guess this is the way most hands tend to be, contrary to rumors.

I. What Happened:

A. The bidding:

With eight highs in first position, I pass, of course.

East
♠ 6 4
♥ J 6 3 2
♦ A 7 3 2
♣ K 10 7

South opens the bidding with a call of one diamond. Partner shows life with an overcall of one spade. North bids two clubs and South bids 2NT. North then bids three diamonds, which buys the contract. It looks like we're out with a whimper.

The Bidding

N	E	S	W
	pass	1D	1S
2C	pass	2NT	pass
3D	all pass		

B. The play:

Partner leads the seven of hearts as dummy comes down:

North (dummy)
♠ 10 7
♥ K 10 8
♦ Q 5 4
♣ A J 9 5 3

East (me)
♠ 6 4
♥ J 6 3 2
♦ A 7 3 2
♣ K 10 7

The eight is played from dummy, and I play the jack which loses to the queen. Declarer then leads the six of diamonds to the queen and my ace. Back comes the six of spades which is won by partner's queen. Partner then returns the four of hearts which is won by declarer in dummy with the king. The ten of spades then goes to the ace of declarer. The jack of spades is covered by partner's king and ruffed in dummy and overruffed by me. I then give partner the obvious heart ruff. Partner returns a club which is ducked by dummy and won by my king. That ends the carnage . . . down one. We got a spade, a diamond, a club, a spade ruff and a heart ruff.

C. Results:

We end the 52 hands with a clear top. How nice! It turns out it did not matter if they made it or not. We would still have a top. They simply failed to get to game. On the last hand, it was the bidding and not the play that determined how well we did. How very fitting. . . .

North (dummy)
♠ 10 7
♥ K 10 8
♦ Q 5 4
♣ A J 9 5 3

West (Jo)
♠ K Q 9 8 3 2
♥ 7 4
♦ 10 8
♣ Q 8 2

East (me)
♠ 6 4
♥ J 6 3 2
♦ A 7 3 2
♣ K 10 7

South (declarer)
♠ A J 5
♥ A Q 9 5
♦ K J 9 6
♣ 6 4

North-South Pair Number	Contract	Made	Down	East-West Points	East-West Matchpoints
1.	3NTS	4		-630	1
2.	3NTS	4		-630	1
3.	3NTS	3		-600	4
4.	3NTS	3		-600	4
5.	3NTS	3		-600	4
6. (us)	3DS		1	+100	6
7.	3NTS	4		-630	1

Apparently, the South bidders opened with 1NT except for our opponent. I can see the bidding going 1NT-3NT. Period. It is possible that the pair we played used the weak notrump. They may have fixed themselves by using it.

II. What Should Have Been:

A. The bidding:

Even if South does not open with 1NT, following the double bid by North, South might venture on with a 3NT bid rather than a 2NT bid. At most, he rates to be off only one point. A bit too conservative by South, I believe. North should not, in my opinion, go back to diamonds. After South has shown a very limited hand by his 2NT call, North should pass. The blame, however, goes mostly to South for not placing the contract in game.

B. The play:

Mostly unimportant . . . nothing unusual happened here.

Lessons:

1. Opening 1NT has many advantages over the opening of 1 in a suit.

2. If you hold 15 highs and stops in the other suits, and partner has bid freely at the two level, other things being equal, bidding 3NT as your second bid (following the opening of 1 in a suit), will leave you 1 point short maximum, and will describe your hand fairly accurately to partner. Stopping short of a notrump game with one point short (at most) is often losing strategy at matchpoints.

Before we begin this section, a brief note of explanation is in order. In bridge literature, certain principles have been developed. Some of the hands included in this volume are illustrative of some of those principles. However, some of the hands develop principles which are useful primarily in "club level duplicate bridge" and are not generally found elsewhere in the literature. Therefore, the lesson summary is divided into two parts. The first part is simply a re-statement of the principles found at the end of each hand . . . those which are found in bridge literature elsewhere and apply to bridge generally. The parentheses following each "lesson" indicate the hand or hands which tend to illustrate the point made. (It, of course, also serves as a count as to how often that principle tended to apply to the hands).

The second part of the lesson summary, as well as the "data examination", might be considered to be the conclusions of this study. The first part of the conclusions include "lessons" which have been found (through the 52 hands) to have been useful in "club level duplicate bridge." The second part of the conclusions examines the data in a different way.

Now then, let's first take a look at some of the principles in general bridge literature which tend to be illustrated by the hands we played.

III. LESSON SUMMARY
PART I

A. The Bidding:

1. Opening with a bid of 1NT, when possible, offers many advantages over the opening of 1 of a suit (#'s 16, 22, 30, 38, 52). There are a variety of gadgets which can be used (such as transfers, Lebensohl, etc.), which are available after a notrump opener but which cannot be used following the opening of one of a suit. Further, there is a certain specificity to the bid which enables partner to place the contract or to double intereference.

2. Once you make a bid describing, within narrow limits, what your hand contains, it is bad policy to make another bid describing the same thing to partner (#'s 17, 46). The captaincy of the hand has then shifted to partner, and he should be making decisions as to the placing of the contract (unless you are invited back into the auction). With that in mind. . .

3. The partner of the notrump opener should make most of the decisions about the placing of the contract or the doubling of the opposition, unless the notrumper is asked to make a decision (#34).

4. Open with a bid of 1NT only if you have stops in at least 3 suits. It is not enough to have balance and 15-17 points. You usually will need to have 3 suits stopped (#26).

5. If you open in a major suit and get a direct raise (playing standard) to 2 of your major, issue an invita-

tion to game when holding 17 or more points (17-18) and pass otherwise (#48).

6. Play in major suits rather than minors even when you have more cards between you and partner in the minors, presuming that you have eight or so cards in the major (#20).

7. A 4-4 major suit fit is preferred over notrump if one or both of the hands is unbalanced and you have a strong major suit holding (#30).

8. When you hold the master suit (spades), it is not necessary to jump in the bidding if you have the points. You will always be able to outbid your opposition because you hold the highest ranking suit (#36).

9. With a 5-3 major suit fit, balance in dummy (no ruffing power), the other suits well stopped, and no dummy reversal possible, often 3NT will be a better contract in a pair game (#'s 5, 42).

10. When your partner repeats his major suit opening, don't persist with your minor if you have two card support for his major (#44).

11. It might be considered mandatory to respond to an opening bid when you hold six high card points (#40).

12. When you describe your hand in terms of point count and in terms of distribution, and partner continues to bid his suit, it is often a good idea to pass and let him play it in his suit (#37).

13. When you know you have the points for game, and the suit, place the contract where it ought to be (#'s 44, 45).

14. Opening the bidding light in first or second position may be deceiving to partner and should be avoided (#14).

15. When partner preempts, it is often right just to pass (#23).

16. To convert partner's vulnerable minor suit, preempt to the five level (and game), you need 3-4 quick

tricks outside the trump suit. To convert the preempt to 3NT, you need 2 tricks outside the trump suit and all other suits stopped, as well as access to the long suit of partner. This presumes a vulnerable preempt, which requires a nearly solid suit, or at least one which would not disappoint partner were he to convert to 3NT (#25).

17. Never preempt in first or second position with a side four card major (#31).

18. After partner preempts, converting to 3NT with a singleton in a side suit is suicidal, unless that singleton is the ace (#31).

19. Generally, prefer to take a chance at notrump, rather than game in a minor, if all suits appear to be stopped (#38).

20. In the pass out seat, one should pass unless one holds a total of 15 points (counting the number of high card points + the number of spades held on one's hand) (#43).

In terms of competitive bidding, the following might be said:

21. When the opposition is about to play in one of a minor, and your side holds both majors, don't let them buy the contract at the one level (#4).

22. More generally, don't let them buy the contract at the one level (in a suit) unless you hold a stack in their suit (#7).

23. If you sense that the hand is a misfit, let them buy the contract (#10).

24. If points seem to be evenly distributed between the two sides, play to get a plus score (#11).

25. When points seem to be evenly distributed between the two sides, and you hold queens and jacks for your points and length in their suit, your holding often calls for defense rather than offense (#11).

26. With a strong playing hand and no wasted values in the opponents' suits, don't sell out too cheaply (#36).

27. When you and your partner agree on a suit, as does the opposition, don't let them buy the contract on the two level, although be careful vulnerable against non-vulnerable (#43).

28. When your opponents are vulnerable and are bidding and your side is not vulnerable, interfering at low levels may prevent them from perfectly describing their hands to each other, and therefore they may not reach the ideal contract (#15).

29. With a strong playing hand and no wasted values in the opponents' suits, don't sell out too cheaply (#36).

30. When you are non-vulnerable (against weak opposition) and your RHO opens 1NT, it may be a good idea to stick in a bid if you have little defense and a decent suit (#47).

31. When the opposition opens up with 1NT, and you are vulnerable and have a nice suit, it sometimes pays to pass. You may end up on lead against a notrump contract and have the perfect lead (#49).

32. Doubling voluntarily bid games offers little matchpoint advantage (#2).

33. When, in direct position, you double a notrump opener (indicating an equivalent hand), the responder to the double should strongly consider passing if the majority of the points belong to your side (particularly if they are vulnerable) (#24).

34. When your side has the majority of points, but you have no clear bid, it may be right just to pass and or double your opponents (#32).

35. When you voluntarily bid game and your opponents outbid you, a pass following the opponent's bid is forcing. The partner of the passer must double or bid on (#51).

36. When you don't want your partner to continue to compete in the auction, and you can set them, you think,

doubling their last bid is a sign to partner not to continue (#51).

Now, let's take a look at some of the lessons learned in terms of defense.

B. The Defense :

1. Generally, it is preferable to lead suits they did not bid rather than the suits that they did bid. (#6).
2. It is usually a good idea to lead trumps if your side has the balance of points, dummy is weak, declarer is two suited, and you have the side suit well stopped (#8). (How is that for something specific? If you ever run into it, let me know.)
3. Typically, it is bad to lead queen from Q-X in an off suit. The same is true for J-X (#23).
4. When leading against notrump, it is bad generally to lead fourth best from a four card tenace holding such as A-Q-X-X. Another suit should be led (#28).
5. When you think that you have no good lead to make against notrump, lead the suit and the card which will mislead partner the least (#41).
6. Generally, it is bad to lead out the ace (unsupported) of a suit you and your partner have bid. Periodically, the person to your right (the declarer) may have an honor in the suit, like the king, and you will have given him a trick. The same cannot be easily said for the lead of a king or queen (#47). (Like may of the other statements made here, there are many exceptions to this rule.)
7. When dummy has an established suit (or an establishable one), it is necessary to break declarer's communications with the dummy. Failing to be able to do that, it is a good idea to cash out (#18). And, a corollary
. . .
8. When, on defense, you see no chance of getting any

more tricks, cash out (#41).

9. When, on defense, you have long trumps, it is often, though not always, a good idea not to overruff declarer (#21).

10. When the opposition opens one notrump, and later gets the contract, the specificity of the notrump bid will, as the hand progresses, enable you to place certain cards in partner's hand and thereby find the most productive defense (#22).

11. When the declarer in notrump fails to begin by attacking a suit, there is usually a reason why he fails to do so. It may be either he has that suit well under control or he is hurting in that suit. In either case, deciding which (if it is one of the two) will give you a key to the proper defense (#27).

12. If you can figure out what declarer is likely to do on offense, do the opposite and you will often have found the best defense (#10).

13. If you think that declarer is likely to make a certain play, plan ahead how you will respond so that hesitation at that moment won't give you away (#19).

14. When you hold the queen-jack in a suit in which, by his lead, partner has indicated the holding of the top two honors, drop the queen on the first card (such as on the king if he leads king from ace-king) so that partner may underlead his ace to reach your hand (#37).

15. Sophisticated defensive techniques do help in getting the most out of a hand, although they may not be used very often (#46).

If I haven't bored you entirely with this list, let's look at the last category, the play of the hand.

C. The Play:

1. In a trump contract, when you hold a long, non-runable side suit, one of the first things you should consider is the ruffing of that suit in dummy (#35).

2. If you are trying to decide which way to finesse (you have an option), finesse in the direction in which, if it loses, the winner of the trick will do less damage than would be done if the other person were in the lead (assuming the lack of any other information, of course) (#50).

3. When you hold the queen in one hand and the jack in another, let the opposition break the suit, which will guarantee you a trick (or at least a stop in the suit) (#47).

4. The timing of the hand should be planned before the play to trick one (#45).

5. The communication between declarer and dummy must be constantly kept in mind (#47).

6. When you think that you can make the requisite number of tricks for your contract, then is the time to think of ways in which overtricks might be had (#50).

7. When your contract appears to be doomed, to avoid a bigger set, cash out (#26).

8. When you need one trick more than you can see, run off your winners. That may have the effect (against non-experts particularly) of making them think a squeeze is operating. They may pitch the wrong card (#25).

9. The opening lead often provides the key to the opponents' hands in terms of distribution. It gives the declarer a clue about how he should play the hand. The opening lead ought to be thought about before the play to the first trick (#17).

10. Most non-experts, when defending against a suit contract will, almost automatically, lead their short suits. That will provide a clue to the declarer (#21).

Conclusions

IV. Lesson Summary Part II

1. Bidding is particularly that which determines how well you do in the local game. To give you an idea of just how preeminent bidding happens to be, consider the following: Of the 52 hands played, the bidding was determinative, in terms of the matchpointing, in 29 hands. The bidding and the play together affected the matchpointing in 21 hands (with the bidding being the more important), and in only 2 of the 52 hands was the declarer play or the defense what mattered in terms of how well a pair happened to do. What this means to me, then, is that to improve your game for local play, time should be spent perfecting the sophistication of your bidding techniques. That means that bids made, when they are perfected, have more narrowly defined limits and meanings than do those bids not perfected. Much less time, if time and energy are at all a factor, should be spent on declarer play and defense. This author realizes that the latter two elements are those which tend to be the most interesting to most people. Perhaps that is why there are so many books out which deal with declarer play and defense . . . people like to read about those things.

2. If you consider a game bid to be marginal, it is best

not to bid it . . . play in the partial (#'s 3, 16, 33, 35, 49).

3. If you consider a slam bid to be marginal , it is best to settle for the game and not bid the slam (#'s 9, 13, 29).

4. And, finally, when you happen to be playing in a partial, it is very important to just get a plus score (#12). Your first obligation is to make your contract.

V. Data examination:

1. High card points:

Over the course of the 52 hands, I had, believe it or not, an average of 10.0 points/hand. Jo (and also Artie, Bucky and Lloyd) had an average of 10.2 points/hand. Apparently, in this respect, these 52 hands were quite representative of hands in general. Interestingly, I had only one hand over 17 high card points and Jo had none over 18. Similarly, neither of us had a yarborough. 94.3% of all our hands were between 16-3 HCP's, 83.7% between 15 and 6, 61.6% between 13 and 7, and 46.2% (almost half) between 8 and 12 points . . . a bidding range. If we are dealing with a bell shaped curve, that means that the peak is high and the ends flatten out quickly. To me this indicates that extraordinary amounts of time ought not be spend perfecting bidding systems that deal with large hands. More time ought to be spent dealing with hands in the average range.

In terms of our combined holdings on each hand: in no case did we have a high card total of less than 10, or more than 30. If we are dealing with a theoretical 33 points for 6NT, it did not even come up — not even close. Only 13% of all the hands were in the 26+ range (which is normally considered to be the game range). Similarly, only 10% of our holdings were in the 14 and below range. That means that 77% of our hands were in the 15-25 point range. Being even more specific, 54% (over half of our hands) were between 17-23 points. That means that most hands could be expected to be competitive in terms of bidding. Therefore, sharpening competitive bidding skills would seem to be very important, rather than the tuning of slam techniques (which, incidentally, occupy much of bridge columns' space).

Or, dealing slightly differently with some of the data above, 23% of all hands tended to be in the 26 and above range for one of the pairs. But, 38% of all hands are in the 25 and above range. However, high card points are not the only story. Let's take a look at distribution points.

2. Distribution points:

People count distribution points in a variety of ways, of course. The method I used to tabulate the following is this: When you have a holding of A-K in a suit, you can count 1½ points. For Q-X or J-X or K-X, you get ½ point. For queen or jack stiff, you get 1½ points. For queen-jack bare you get no points. For ace bare you get 3 points. The rest was standard. Now, I know that distribution points change throughout the hand as you re-evaluate based upon the bidding. However, a priori (before any bidding) and based upon the above, Jo and I each averaged 1.2 distribution points per hand.

If we say it takes 26 points to make a game in a major, and if that includes distribution points, and if the average in distribution points per partnership is 2.4/hand, then it really takes only 23.6 high card points to make a game in a major, barring overlap in points, etc. With that in mind, we note that 52% of all hands were in the 23.6 plus range. However, a much smaller percentage would contain the above numbers and at the same time have a major suit fit. We shall later see that 46% of all bids made on the 52 hands were game bids. Locating that major suit fit would seem to be important. However, we noted earlier that not bidding marginal games was winning strategy.

3. Suit length:

To my surprise, there was quite a bit of consistency in suit length, contrary to what I have seen in "random" computer hands. I averaged, for the longest suit in my hand, 4.75 cards. Jo and my other partners averaged 4.77 cards/hand. Neither of us had a suit of more than seven cards. The shortest was, of course, four cards long. Only 16% of all hands contained a suit 6 or 7 cards long (13% - 6 cards long and 3% - 7 cards long). There were more hands with flat distribution (no suit longer than four cards long) than there were hands which held suits of five cards in length.

We can therefore expect many hands with 4-4 major suit fits. More specifically, we can expect many hands with 4-4 major suit fits with 7-9 points or 7-10 points in one of the hands. Therefore, negative doubles and forcing notrumps would seem to be much needed tools. With nine points and four hearts, after an opening of one spade, one can hardly bid two hearts. Bidding techniques like negative doubles need to be incorporated into one's system to take advantage of these numbers (in terms of making it more likely to uncover the 4-4 fits and in terms of being specific about the 5-3 fits).

4. Points in the plus column:

For the first 26 weeks, Jo and I had 10 plus scores and 16 minus scores. For the second 26 weeks we had 17 plus scores and 9 minus scores (of the 52 hands). Or, in terms of percentages: For the first 26 weeks we had a 47.4% game going (pretty miserable) while for the last 26 we had a 65.5% game going. I think we started to learn something from having analyzed these hands. We had 5 zeros the first 26 and no zeros the last 26.

Let's deal with the pluses and what that means. When you make your bid or set your opponent, you get a plus. When we got pluses, we were 85% in the above average range (in terms of matchpointing). Sixty-eight percent of all minuses tend to be below average in terms of matchpointing. Translated: when you have a lot of pluses in a local game, you have probably had a good game. There is an 85% chance that the plus is an above average board for you. The name of the game, then, is getting pluses (getting a score on your side of the ledger). That may mean that if they had a two level contract, which they rate to make, you might as well balance. Try to get them one level higher and make it a bit more difficult for them to make their bid. Even sticking a bid in for lead directing purposes will often give you an edge and an increased chance of setting the contract.

5. Bids made:

There were 346 bids at our club over the last year. Of that number, 217 were made or were made with overtricks. That means that 63% of all bids were made here. Let's examine that more specifically.

6. Two level bids made:

There were 62 two level bids and, of those, 37 were made . . . a 60% rate.

7. Three level bids made:

There were 68 three level bids (not including game bids) and, of those, 40 were made . . . a 59% rate.

8. Four level bids:

For minor suits only, there were 8 four level bids and 4 of those were made for a 50% rate.

9. Game bids that were made:

There were 159 game bids, of which 105 were made, a 66% rate of success.

10. Slams bid:

We only had 6 slams bid, of which 2 made . . . a 33% rate. This does not include slam bids which were obvious sacrifices.

11. Slam sacrifices:

There were 2 slam sacrifices bid. In one of the two cases (50%), the sacrificer got a better than average board.

What then can we say about the above information (#'s 5-11)? It is apparent that there is little difference between the success rate for two level bids and those for three level bids (60% vs. 59%). That, however, flies in the face of the conventional wisdom (note Mike Lawrence's book on balancing) and this author's experience. This author notes that when the opponents are forced to the three level, they will periodically miss making their contracts by one trick. If they were not so forced, they would have a plus score rather than a minus score. Furthermore, because they rate to make a two level contract (the points are, after all, fairly evenly distributed between the two sides and they get to name the trump suit), it does little harm to bid or try and find a suit . . . which will at least force them to the three level. Furthermore, when you balance you will periodically buy the contract and perhaps get a plus or at least a smaller minus.

In any event, a minus because they made two and a minus for having gone down one vulnerable are both minuses. And, if they can make two in a major and you go down one vulnerable, not doubled, you have done something significant in terms of matchpointing. The name of the game is balance.

And, if they bid, voluntarily, a game in a major, vulnerable, they have a 66% chance of making it. If you have a suit, non-vulnerable, you may be better off bidding to the five level rather than letting them make their game. That depends, of course, upon the strength of your suit and your defensive and offensive potential. Judgment counts here.

By contrast, if they bid a slam, there is no need to double. Very few others will be in that slam. So, if they go down, you will get a good board anyhow. And, they only have a 33% chance of making it. Just don't give away any tricks. Make them make it.

As for slam sacrifices against other slams . . . If they have a 33% chance, it is a bit risky, although 1 of the 2 slam sacrifices resulted in a good board for the sacrificers. You must have a very good idea that they are cold for it before taking that chance.

But, we have some more information: What are the chances of getting points in the plus column for playing a hand relative to the chances of getting pluses for defending?

12. Pluses for defending:

People who held the hands we did for all 52 hands (including ourselves) defended 173 times and got pluses 63 of those times. That means that the chance of getting a plus for defending is 36%. Almost 2/3 of the time, when you are defending, you are doomed for a minus score. We already know that when you have points in the minus column you have a much better than average chance of getting a below average board.

And . . .

13. Pluses for playing:

In terms of playing, people (including ourselves) played 172 times and had pluses 107 of those. That means that the chance of getting a number in the plus column is 62% when you play the hand. Numbers in the plus column have an 85% chance of being above average. Need I say more? Yes, perhaps I ought to spell that out.

When you play the hand, you have a much better chance of getting an above average board than when your opponents play the board. Therefore, don't let them buy the contract too easily. At least force them to the three level, or even higher. What have you got to lose? Non-experts rarely do that. It certainly appears to be winning strategy.

Skeptics among you are probably gritting their teeth and asking, "What about the chances of getting doubled?"

13. Two level doubles:
There were seven doubles on the two level and six succeeded in setting the contract. (Of course, down one nonvulnerable may result in a good board.)

14. Three level doubles:
There were three doubles on the three level and all resulted in sets.

15. Four level doubles:
There were six doubles on the four level and three of those six were set.

16. Five level doubles:
There were six doubles on the five level and three of those were set.

17. Six level doubles:
There were three doubles on the six level and all were set.

That means that, for two and three level doubles, nine out of ten were set. For doubles of the four level and above, nine out of 15 were set (60%).

We are particularly interested in two and three level doubles, of course, because most hands are competitive in terms of bidding. The points on most hands, as we have seen, are fairly evenly distributed between the two sides, so the paramount question is to bid or not to bid (in terms of the likelihood of getting a minus or a plus). First of all, we have seen that there were 130 bids (not including game bids) on the two and three levels. Of those 130, 10 were doubled. That is only 8%. And, 59.5% of the two and three level bids were made. Therefore, given the small chance of being doubled and the likelihood of the opponents' contract making, the fear of the double should not prevent you from competing. Chances are, you won't get doubled. And 10% of the time that you are, you will make it. And, of the nine that were set, one resulted in a good board for the bidder. The name of the game, then is don't be afraid to bid on. The other half of the coin, of course, is that you should not be afraid to double. You have a good chance of setting them, if you think you will. And, if you just let them play the contract, they have a good chance of getting a good board. You might as well bid. Of course, in the local, non-expert game, there is much less competition on low levels than you would find in tournaments. That is what makes the strategies very different and a separate publication necessary.

VI. Score Examination

As we have seen, having a score in the plus column will give one an 85% chance of having an above average board. Given the close association between pluses and scores, I felt it ought to be possible to devise a formula with which one can predict what kind of game one had (or is having) before the scores are tabulated. Certainly, if one does this prior to the last round, for example, one would, if the formula is accurate, be able to determine if one needs to press for top boards or just "stay in your seat." In other words, a formula based upon the number of pluses compared to the total number of boards played should provide a reasonable estimate of how one is doing . . . because there is such a strong relationship between pluses and above average boards.

The formula which I developed is applicable to club level as well as tournament bridge, although the "constant" would have to be altered, depending upon the type of game.

To estimate one's score:

1. Use the following formula:

$\dfrac{\text{number of pluses}}{\text{Total number of boards played}}$ times ("constant") times

(Total possible score) = Predicted Score

Or, count up how many times (of the hands played) you got points in the plus column and divide that number by the total number of boards played. Multiply the product by the "constant" and multiply that product by the total possible score to that point. That will give you an estimate of how you are doing to that point.

But, how does one develop the constant?

2. To develop the constant:

It will take several sessions of bridge before one is able to arrive at a reliable constant, which can be used from then on. It is necessary to work backwards. At the end of an evening, find out one's score. Put that score into the formula, along with the other "knowns." Transfer the "knowns" to one side of the formula and solve for "X", the constant. For example, if, in one evening, you had a score of 90 on an average of 84 (top of 168), you would do the following (presuming you had, for example, 15 pluses out of 24 boards):

$$\frac{15}{24} \text{ times (``X'') times (168)} = 90$$

so,

(.625) times ("X") times (168) = 90

("X") times (.625 times 168) = 90

("X") times (105) = 90

$$\text{``X''} = \frac{90}{105}$$

"X" = .8571

In other words, you have developed a constant of .8571 for that evening. Then, if you do that for ten evenings, you will get a variety of constants. After you arrange the ten from highest to lowest, take the average of the middle two to get your working constant.

You are then ready to use the formula, using the constant which you have developed. Just plug in the number on a given evening.

3. The question is, just how utilitarian is it? That depends upon the game and its regularity. I would expect that tournaments would be much more predictable than club level games, though I do not know that for a fact. This formula was being developed just as this book was going to press and is not yet completely tested . . . in terms of its utility.

It is also the case that your margin of error may be quite great. One must realize that the prediction of the formula might be said to predict within a range . . . not an actual score. For example, after you have plugged into the formula, you will get your expected predicted score. If you then repeat the process using your second highest constant and your second lowest constant, you will have developed three predicted scores. Chances are 80% that your actual score will fall within the range of the three scores, with the one in the middle probably being closest to the actual.

4. Now that you have digested the formula to this point, let us make the entire equation more accurate. Certainly, passed out boards and those on which you got clear tops or clear bottoms will alter the predictability. A score of -1100 for example (down 4 doubled and vulnerable) is probably a bottom or near bottom in most cases. It would just appear as a minus on your ledger, but, in reality, is more than just a minus. Therefore, to be really accurate, it is necessary to take "clear bottoms or near clear bottoms" and "clear tops or near clear tops" and "passed out boards" out of the formula. How we do that is this: During the ten weeks of the formula development (or ten sessions), do not include passed out boards (P) or near clear tops (T) or near clear bottoms (B), only other boards. Keep track of these during each evening. Your constant will then pertain only to boards which are not one of the

three listed exceptions. You must, of course, for any given week of constant development, reduce the total number of boards played and the total possible score correspondingly. So, if you had 1 passed out board and 2 clear tops and 1 clear bottom, and there were 24 boards in play that evening, with a top on a board of 7, the total number of boards (for the purpose of determining the overall constant) would be 20 and the total possible score would be 20 times 7 = 140. Get it?

5. Now for an example:

Suppose you have thus worked up a constant of .9206. Your second highest constant is .9948 and your second lowest constant is .8675. One evening you played 28 boards with a top of 6 on a board. During that round you passed one out and are pretty sure you had two clear tops (or near tops) and one clear bottom (or near bottom). Of the 24 remaining boards, you had 14 pluses and 10 minuses. What do you predict your score to be?

The formula:

$$\frac{\text{\# of pluses}}{\text{total number of boards}} \times \text{constant} \times \text{total possible score} = \text{predicted score}$$

$$\frac{14}{24} \times .9206 \times (24 \times 7) = \text{predicted score}$$

$$.5833 \times .9206 \times 168 = \text{predicted score}$$

$$.5370 \times 168 = \text{score}$$

$$90.22 = \text{score}$$

Now, we have to reconsider the passed out board and the two tops and one bottom. Add one half of a top for the passed out board and "a top" for every top and "0" for every bottom. So, in this case, add "3½" for the passed out, "14" for the two tops and "0" for the bottom. Your final predicted score will be 90.22 + 3½ + 14 =

330

107.72 on a top of 196 (28 times 7). That is a 55% game. Now, repeat the process with the second highest and second lowest constants.

With the second highest:

.5833 X .9948 X 168 = 97.48

Add the same 3½ and 14 to this: 114.98. This is an estimate of a 59% game.

With the second lowest constant:

.5833 X .8675 X 168 = 85.01

Add the 3½ and 14 to get 102.51 (a 52% game).

Chances are 80% that you have a game in between 102.5 and 115 on a top of 196, with a score of 107.5 being probably closest to the actual.

If you use more than ten constant development sessions, of course, you will be much more accurate in your prediction. Furthermore, if you use the third highest and third lowest constants to find your range, when you include more than ten sessions to develop your constant, you will be much more precise. In any event, it is a start, and one which I perceive to be potentially useful.

I think one final additional point needs to be made. The constants which are developed are specific to a particular partnership. Because some partnerships are better at declarer play or defense or bidding than others, getting a plus or a minus to one partnership may not mean the same as to another. Each person should keep a record on each partner he/she has with separate constants for each.

Right now, it may seem a bit complex. However, when you do get the constant, the entire process will take about 30 seconds, believe it or not (using a pocket calculator), to predict your score.

Dr. Mark Routman is a sociology professor at Delta State University in Mississippi. He claims to have learned the essentials of Bridge from his mother, but never seriously entered competitive Bridge until 1978. He is an Advanced Senior Master and is in the process of obtaining his Life Master rank. He was recently named Player of the Year by the Cleveland, MS Bridge Club.